THE LIBRARY
ST. MARY'S COLLEGE OF MARYLAND
ST. MARY'S CITY, MARYLAND 20686

THE MAGIC CITY

J[ames] W[illiam] Buel

ARNO PRESS
A New York Times Company
New York • 1974

Reprint Edition 1974 by Arno Press Inc.

Reprinted from a copy in the University
of Illinois Library

POPULAR CULTURE IN AMERICA: 1800-1925
ISBN for complete set: 0-405-06360-1
See last pages of this volume for titles.

Manufactured in the United States of America

Library of Congress Cataloging in Publication Data

Buel, James William, 1849-1920.
   The magic city.

   (Popular culture in America)
   Reprint of the ed. published by the Historical Pub.
Co., St. Louis, issued in series: Historical fine art
series.
   1. Chicago. World's Columbian exposition, 1893
--Views. I. Title. II. Series.
T500.C1B85 1974   910.93'4'074017311   74-15728
ISBN 0-405-06364-4

2-26-79

.....HISTORICAL FINE ART SERIES.....

THE MAGIC CITY

A MASSIVE PORTFOLIO

OF

Original Photographic Views of the Great World's Fair

AND ITS TREASURES OF ART, INCLUDING A VIVID REPRESENTATION OF THE FAMOUS

Midway Plaisance

WITH GRAPHIC DESCRIPTIONS BY AMERICA'S BRILLIANT HISTORICAL AND DESCRIPTIVE WRITER

J. W. BUEL

A PHOTOGRAPHIC AND HISTORICAL REPRESENTATION OF

THE "MAGIC CITY" BY-THE-LAKE, WITH ITS VAST TREASURES OF THE WORLD'S ART

Reproduced in Splendid Realism, as it was seen by millions of visitors, in a series of

300 Magnificent Photographic Views

PUBLISHED WEEKLY, BY THE

HISTORICAL PUBLISHING COMPANY,

ST. LOUIS, MO.   1894   PHILADELPHIA, PA.

The Engravings in this volume were made from original photographs, and are specially protected by Copyright, and notice is hereby given, that any person or persons guilty of reproducing or infringing the copyright in any way will be dealt with according to law.

Entered, according to Act of Congress, in the year 1894, by
H. S. SMITH,
In the Office of the Librarian of Congress, at Washington, D. C.
All rights reserved.

GATEWAY TO THE MAGIC CITY.

THE GENIE of the lamp, that flashed into creation before the astonished eyes of Aladdin, a palace more gorgeous than all the wealth of a mighty Sultan was able to duplicate, has long ceased to roam the world, the subject of powerful talismans, ravishing the earth of its jewels, the sky of its gems, and the ocean of its treasures; but there are magicians still, who rival the proudest conceptions of imaginary demons with realities as splendid as ever oriental fancy painted. This is not an age of miracles, but it is one of works, in which the powers of human genius transcend the beauty and opulence of Arabic dreams, when the airy unsubstantials of intoxicated reveries seem to be fabricated into living ideals of grandeur more magnificent than any that ever Rajah or Caliph beheld in vision or in fact.

We are grown somewhat accustomed to the marvelous in human achievement, through modern discovery and invention, but these wonders of intellectual activities and original direction usually burst upon us singly, like a meteor leaping across the sky and then plunging into darkness. It was reserved to the Columbian Exposition of 1893, to gather into one incomparable aggregation all the surprises of modern accomplishment, and by such exhibition bring us to a realization of the amazing performances, and a comprehension of the almost boundless capacity of human genius. To this display of artistic handiwork, all the civilized nations of the earth contributed, each in friendly rivalry for reward, each presenting the best examples of their respective products in the arts, mechanical, ideal and industrial. Thus all nations were reflected as in a looking glass, a magic mirror, in which was to be seen, to the highest advantage, every marvel of the age, while the past was here joined to the present by exhibitions of the implements, devices and clumsy inventions that characterized the infancy of America, and the slow evolution of the old world. To be a witness of these masterpieces of inventive ingenuity, and of the displays that dazzled by the miracle of their workmanship as well as by their beauty, contrasted with the products of earlier times, was to live through many centuries, and to be as traveled and old as the Wandering Jew. The sight was like unto a vision that no mortal tongue or pen can describe.

The publishers of this great Portfolio, recognizing the impossibility of conveying, or preserving a satisfactory idea of the Columbian Exposition through historic description alone, adopted the more impressive and attractive method of telling the story in pictures. To photography we owe much, but never was our indebtedness so great as now, when by its aid all the beauties, the grandeur, and the treasures of the World's Fair have been preserved intact, upon which all the eyes of future generations may feast themselves; not upon the mummified remains of the Fair, but upon the entire Exposition as fresh for all time as a rose bathing in the morning dew.

This magic city, reared in a six months, was more than the realized vision of a dreamer, more dazzling than the airy castles of idealism, richer than the palaces of stimulated fancy, and after bewildering the world with its matchless splendors for a six months more, dissolved like a mirage, leaving only its memory, golden and glorious, as an incitation to this and coming generations. But the charm, the witchery, the magnificence of the Fair is preserved by photography, and thus it endures with scarcely diminished lustre as a glorification of the age, as well as an illustrious commemoration of American discovery.

It is a remarkable thing that architecture attained its greatest perfection, if beauty alone be considered, towards the close of the fifteenth century, and contemporary with Columbus. The expulsion of the Moors from Spain was followed by a decline in the constructive art, the practical superseding the ideally beautiful, and so continued until the genius of the Columbian Exposition produced, to our wonderment and admiration, a composite of the most exquisite architecture of the Moors, and the symmetrical and utilitarian construction of the present. Thus the buildings of the Fair exhibit both renascent and original designs, a combination that is at once the amazement of the Old World and the pride of the New.

The groupings of the buildings, the material of their construction, imitative of marble, and the platting of the grounds, were realizations of the highest conception of art, producing a city as beautiful as imagery ever glimpsed, or a dream ever outlined. It was a Heliopolis, grander, more resplendent, more marvelous than that wonderful metropolis of the sun whose Syriac ruins still excite the astonishment of learned men, and was enriched with the world's offerings to an extent that has no parallel in history. And not only was the Columbian Fair a miracle of architecture, and an exhibition of the most remarkable products of all nations in the varied fields of art and industry, of machinery, fabrics, paintings, sculpturing, engineering, and ingenuity, for its fame must be perpetuated by reason of its broad scope in branches of intellectual science, its congresses convened and attended by the masters of the age, whose counsels and suggestions were towards promoting fraternity and human aggrandizement through spiritual, mental and physical development. Object lessons in intellectual advancement were afforded by the gathering here of representatives of many semi- and totally uncivilized races, brought from far away and benighted countries, peoples from hyperborean climes and from Equatorial regions, the extremes of heat and cold, where the savagery of original condition still prevails, among whom superstition controls and cruelty is custom. The Afric cannibal, the Innuit Shamanist, the scarred and tattooed Polynesian, the Indian and the fierce Tartar, were transplantations forming curious and most interesting parts of an ethnographic exhibition such as was never before seen, affording instruction to visitors beyond their ability to otherwise acquire.

The lessons which America, the world, has learned from the Columbian Fair are more priceless than jewels; they have opened our eyes and understanding not only to the capacities of man, but help us to better appreciate the blessings of Christian civilization, and the loving direction and guidance of God. We have been instructed and inspired by the wonders, the beauties, the elevating and the useful displays made by nations and individuals, in all of which we cannot fail to discern a manifestation of beneficence, that divine benevolence, charity and goodness which is leading us surely towards a happier, higher and more righteous condition. The story of the Magic City concludes with a moral that is of infinite value as an incitement to men and women of all creeds and of all nations.

J. W. Buel

ADMINISTRATION BUILDING.—As the Manufactures Building held the wondering interest of multitudes by the unexampled magnitude of its dimensions, so the Administration Building struck with amazement, and won the unstinted admiration of every World's Fair visitor by its incomparable beauty and artistic magnificence. Its cost of $650,000 furnishes a very small idea of the originality and splendor of its design, for it stood as the very embodiment of supreme architectural genius. The honor of its design belongs to Robert M. Hunt, of New York, whose capacity to conceive and ability to execute is now established for all time by this charming example of his work. The building occupied a square of 262 feet, with square Doric pavilions on the corners, between which were as many arched entrances to the rotunda. Upon the inner corners of these four-storied pavilions, and around the rotunda, rested an octagonal Ionic superstructure with columnar supports, on the corners of which were effigies designed by the greatest sculptors of the age. Surmounting these was the octagonal dome, golden as the sun itself, 260 feet above the ground. At night the building was lighted by means of 5000 electric globes, and the effect, as may be imagined, was that of unspeakable splendor. The interior was in every respect as artistic and beautiful as the exterior. Six large elevators carried visitors to the upper stories, whence imposing views of the surrounding grounds were had. The vault of the dome was beautified by Dodge, with allegorical paintings appropriate to the occasion, commemorative of the progress of the age no less than of the Columbian discovery, while the panels, both inside and out, were ornamented with suitable inscriptions. The Administration Building, as its name implies, was used by the administrative officers of the Exposition, and the appointments of the quarters were as elegant as the building itself.

THE LAPLAND VILLAGE.—From the land of ice and snow, the extreme northwest of the Czar's dominion, the sterile territory of the reindeers, came a company of Laplanders to swell the attractions of Midway Plaisance, bringing with them their full regalias of neck comforters and felt boots, and a complement of camp paraphernalia. They were curious folks to people who through a sight of these hardy Northmen were first introduced to the customs of those who dwell near the icy cape. These Laplanders were specimens of a remarkably brave race who fought under Charles XII. against overwhelming forces of Peter the Great, nor surrendered their liberties until decimation, almost annihilation, compelled them to cease the unequal struggle. The Lap Village at the World's Fair was a realistic reproduction of a native community. There was a conical dirt covered hut, with an opening in the centre to permit the smoke to escape, bunks for sleeping quarters, and the narrow walls hung with trophies of the chase. There was also a Lapland mother with her infant swathed in heavy clothes and deer skins, and equally realistic was the reindeer corral in which a herd of those animals was kept and used to draw a fur-clothed native in a canoe-sled around the enclosure. These exhibitions of reindeer sledding were more comical than illustrative, for while a sled made of a hollow log may answer the purpose admirably on deep snow, it is an insecure vehicle on dry ground, and doubly so when drawn by a jumping deer that turns corners so sharply as to send the sled and occupant rolling over and over like an end boy on the string in the play of "cracking the whip."

CHICAGO DAY AT THE EXPOSITION.—Never before in the history of the world was there such a crowd as was drawn to the World's Fair on October 9th, the anniversary of the great fire in Chicago in 1871. Immense preparations had been made in anticipation of an unprecedented number of visitors, these preparations consisting of programs that would provide the most impressive as well as the most interesting entertainment. Twenty-two years had passed since the demon of destruction enveloped with his fiery wings the young metropolis of the West, and left it a giant heap of embers. But from these ashes rose, phœnix-like, a greater city, purified by flame, strengthened by calamity, invigorated by ordeal. Chicago resolved to celebrate her resurrection, to commemorate her achievements, to mingle her gladness with the praise offerings of the world. People gathered there from every point of the compass to take part in the rejoicing, and the citizens opened their treasuries of wealth to make the triumphant jubilation an occasion of unexampled splendor. The city was accordingly bedecked like a bride, and the celebration was made a festival of exultation. A tremendous procession, martial, commercial, and civilian, paraded the streets with what appeared an endless line of allegoric floats, and banners waved everywhere, the insignia of patriotic pride. The joyful multitudes poured into the Exposition grounds until the six hundred and thirty-three acres could scarcely accommodate any more. The record of the day showed 751,000 admissions, more than double the number of persons that attended the great Paris Exposition on any one day. The photograph herewith exhibits the crowd as it appeared in and around the Administration Building and the Court of Honor on the ever memorable 9th of October, 1893. Such a sight will hardly be witnessed again.

AN EAST VIEW FROM MACMONNIES' COLUMBIAN FOUNTAIN.—The supreme example of statuary art at the Exposition, the chef d'œuvre of allegoric representation at the Fair, was concededly that designed by Frederick MacMonnies as a heroic centrepiece to the Court of Honor. Our view here is a general one, showing less of the Columbian Fountain, which is dimmed by the long perspective. The expansive view afforded from the Administration Building east was one of marvelous splendor. Straight across the lagoon, at the east extremity, stood the colossal statue of the Republic, with the beautiful Arch of Triumph and Peristyle as a background; on the south, its long front facing the lagoon, was Machinery Building, while the north boundary of the view presents the south end and charming loggia of Manufactures Building. In the Court of Honor was a music pavilion, near MacMonnies' Fountain, in which a series of concerts were given daily, thus combining music and art in a realism of the most entrancing and charming conception. It was a very paradise of artistic splendor, a substantial dream of opulent magnificence, an inspiration transformed into sumptuous reality.

VIEW OF THE MANUFACTURES AND FISHERIES BUILDINGS.—While the sight of any single building on the grounds was instructive and often inspiring, a full sweep in any direction, taking in a combination of buildings, lagoon, statues, and a hive of human beings, was impressive for its grandeur and picturesqueness. The view northeasterly, as shown above, was particularly charming, as, turning from the glare and statuary decorations and ornamentations about the Court of Honor, the visitor's eye wandered among quieter but a scarcely less charming diversity of landscape, along the graceful lagoon and its verdant shores, by the great Manufactures Hall, across Wooded Island, and then rested on the many towered and circular terminals of the Fisheries Building. There was a subdued beauty about the perspective which this sight afforded, the result of pleasing contrast, but the impression was that of dreamy magnificence, of contentful contemplation, of idyllic repose.

THE WOMAN'S BUILDING.—The first full, complete representation ever accorded to woman by this government was at the Columbian Exposition. Her recognition as a part of the body politic, instead of a mere social integer, was made by Congress, through legislative provision that gave to women a magnificent building wherein to hold their councils, and appointed a Board of Lady Managers who exercised the functions of administration and control. To Miss Sophia Hayden, of Boston, was given the honor and emolument of designing and superintending the erection of the Woman's Building, who discharged her part as designer and builder so creditably that the structure was a model of beauty and adaptability, though its cost was only $138,000. Its dimensions were 200 by 388 feet, and two stories high. The building is upon the Renaissance order as to the front exterior, but otherwise is a modern type, especially the asssembly hall which was commodious, and its acoustics excellent. The building was ornamented with many splendid pieces of statuary modeled by Miss Alice Rideout, of California, and some of the interior decorations and paintings were by the hands of distinguished women, among whom was the lamented Russian artist-novelist, Marie Bashkirtseff and the wife of sculptor MacMonnies, and others of scarcely less fame. The last nail driven in the building was composed of gold, silver and copper, and was presented by the people of Montana.

THE ART PALACE.—This beautiful structure was of the Grecian-Ionic style of the most refined classic type, particularly appropriate for the uses to which it was devoted. The building covered an area of 300 by 500 feet, and was intersected at the cardinal points by a grand nave, at the centre of which was a transcept 100 feet wide and 70 feet high, terminating in a dome 60 feet in diameter and 125 feet high, upon the apex of which was a winged figure of victory. Under the grand nave and dome, that flooded the central section with light, the collections of sculpture were displayed. Around the entire building extended a continuous gallery 40 feet wide that furnished at once a delightful promenade and splendid view of the large exhibits. Connected with the main building were two annexes, 120 by 200 feet wide, with colonnades on the three sides of each, from which an excellent view of the grounds was obtained. Though the building was temporary, the immense value of the exhibits it was to contain made it necessary to construct it as nearly fire-proof as possible. Every civilized nation was represented in the collections of statuary and paintings, the number of pieces exhibited being nearly 25,000, of a value approximating $5,000,000, comprising the largest art exhibition ever made in the history of the world. The cost of the building was $600,000.

DAHOMEY CANNIBALS.—It was a strange but purely scientific motive that prompted the bringing from Africa of a company of savage Dahomians, to exhibit them before the sharp and curious gaze of World's Fair visitors. But they afforded a remarkable contrast, the extreme of barbarity in contact with the highest types of civilization. Dahomey is a country of West Africa, noted for the extraordinary valor of its women, who, as Amazons, compose King Behazin's army. Though the Dahomians have been for nearly a century under Arabic influence, and latterly in contact with missionaries as well as with traders and soldiery of England, France and Germany, they have apparently relaxed none of their horrible customs, among which cannibalism is chief. Once every year, during the collection of the annual tax, it is the practice of these savage people to sacrifice a number of prisoners or offenders, whose bodies furnish a feast to the king's followers. So also is it a practice among them to make human sacrifices at the death of their ruler, and in times of great scarcity of food it is common to kill and eat their own kin. As many as forty of these cruel people were brought to the World's Fair, who in a bemba, or village built in imitation of their native homes, gave daily exhibitions of dancing, singing, and their fetish customs. They are a strong, athletic people, possessing much cunning, and considerable intelligence. In appearance, too, they are less forbidding than many other tribes of Africa, and so liberty-loving that they will not submit to slavery, preferring death to servitude.

THE GOVERNMENT BUILDING.—The Government appropriation of $400,000 for a building in which to house its exhibits was wisely expended, as the photograph of that superb structure indicates. The building was of iron, brick, and glass, 420 by 350 feet in size, and two stories in height, with a central octagonal dome 150 feet high. The design was classic, but becomingly plain, as its purpose was more utilitarian than showy. Within the building were exhibits made by the Fish Commission, Smithsonian Institute, and Departments of State, Interior, Agriculture, War, and Post Office, which necessitated the use of a great deal of machinery for the making of cartridges, boring of heavy guns, and the workings of models were a part of the exhibition therein. The building faced the water-front plaza, where were located the life-saving corps, the hospital corps, and batteries of heavy and light field guns and mortars, which appeared to be trained on the battle-ship that lay off shore a short distance. The sight witnessed by visitors approaching the grounds by a lake steamer was decidedly warlike, an effect which was somewhat increased by the Viking ship that was moored to the shore, and which with fierce dragon prow and curved dolphin tail looked like some legendary monster bent on ravage.

GOLDEN PORTAL OF THE TRANSPORTATION BUILDING.—The most pretentious example of architectural display and bewildering effect was unquestionably the central quintuple arched doorway of the Transportation Building, which was made after designs by Adler and Sullivan, of Chicago. The details are both complicated and delicate, and withal rich in design and coloring. Each arch was carefully treated with carvings, or, more properly, bas-reliefs of original patterns, the display being heightened by a symbolic mural painting in the background of the first arch. A square, similarly treated, joined the peripheries of the outer arch, by which the appearance was created, at a distance, of a dazzling picture beautifully framed. The front was painted a delicate pea-green and the bas-relief was overlaid with silver leaf, forming an exquisite combination of color effects, which was still further enhanced by paintings on the arch pedestals.

THE PERISTYLE AND STATUE OF THE REPUBLIC.—Beautiful as a vision conjured under the influence of opalescent skies canopying Oriental sands, was the grand colonnade, or peristyle, which terminated the eastern basin and looked out towards the lake with uplifted white arms in attitude of offering orisons and welcome. It was a dreamland reproduction, to bewilder the sense with unspeakable admiration. In the water-front, facing the inner side of the Peristyle, stood on a lofty pedestal a colossal statue representing the Republic, a master creation wrought by Daniel C. French. The figure was that of a woman draped in the Grecian style, holding in one hand a globe upon which rested an eagle whose outstretched wings symbolized protection. In the other hand was held a pole bearing a liberty cap, significant of the Republic's estimation of freedom. The figure was sixty-five feet high, and was set on a pedestal thirty feet above the water, thus making the total height one hundred feet. It was impossible to correctly estimate the proportions by a view from the grounds, and many ridiculous guesses were therefore made by visitors. The face of the statue was fifteen feet long, the arms thirty feet and the forefingers forty-five inches, and ten inches in diameter. A stairway was built inside the figure, similar to that in the New York statue of Liberty. The total cost was $25,000, the sculptor receiving $8000 for his services, and $1400 was the cost of gilding it.

VIEW OF MANUFACTURES BUILDING FROM THE COURT OF HONOR.—From whatever point of the Fair Grounds the visitor might direct his gaze, it seemed that the huge back of the leviathan building arrested his vision, and compelled him to pause and consider its extraordinary magnitude. Our view above is taken from a position in front of the Administration Building, across the plaza known as the Court of Honor. From this place the great hall of Manufactures and Liberal Arts was especially imposing, not alone for its immensity of size, but also for the symmetry of its proportions, and especially the colonnaded loggia that paralleled the lagoon, suggesting a palace of the Cæsars. Manufactures was separated from the Administration Building by the sinuous lagoon, across which a beautiful bridge was thrown whose arch was high enough to allow ample passageway for gondolas and electric launches. Upon the abutments of the bridge were staff pedestals, on which stood, like sacred animals, twin effigies of buffaloes, representative of the West, mutely sullen, as if challenging the wave of humanity rolling before them.

A BIRD'S-EYE VIEW OF THE WORLD'S FAIR.—That wonder of modern engineering science, the tremendous and dizzy-looking Ferris Wheel, that rotated like some unreal thing in the sky, afforded a panoramic sight more distinct, and almost as expansive, as the Eiffel Tower. In a passenger car hung upon the topmost edge of this cyclopean spider's web, poised 250 feet above the earth, the visitor beheld the Midway Plaisance below him, and a perspective of the World's Fair buildings that was at once beautiful, bewildering, enrapturing. From this top-lofty position our photographic view was taken. The long and broad avenue through the Plaisance is alive with interested spectators, who note with increasing surprise the curious transplantations of peoples and customs from far distant climes to this wonderful gathering place of the world. Towards the right and left are features of Oriental civilization, gilded minarets, where the faithful Moslem uttered his morning and evening prayers, graceful domes, pretty kiosks, a Viennese street and German village, the thatched huts of wild Polynesians, a part of old Egypt, cycloramas, and castles, all in succession, to create a marvelous view of the nations of the earth in a realistic congress. Away in the distance looms against the sky the mastodonic Manufactures Building, and the sun-crowned domes of those great and magnificent structures, the Government and Illinois Buildings, with a faint view of Art Hall on the left. Beyond the White City of art, science and industry, are mistily discerned the blue waters of Lake Michigan, kissing the pale horizon in the receding distance. Such a picture, so glorious, so reflective of the world's progress, so charming with a marvelous diversity and beauty, may never be seen again.

A DETAIL VIEW OF THE PERISTYLE.—One of the finest pieces of renaissant architecture, of the purest Phidian style, was the grand Colonnade, or peristyle, designed as the main entering way to the Fair from the lake. The Corinthian columns were forty-eight in number, representing the States and Territories of the Union, and extended to and connected with the Casino building on the south and Music Hall on the north. On the balustrade were double rows of heroic figures, symbolizing the arts and sciences. The main portal constituted the arch of triumph, on the top of which was placed the Columbian quadriga, or four-horse chariot, designed by French & Potter, and completed at an expense of $15,000. The groups on the pedestals of the arch represent the "Genius of Navigation," and were made after designs by Bela G. Pratt, whose previous artistic creations in sculpture had established his reputation on both hemispheres. The names of five great explorers appeared on the pediment, and the glory of national achievement was proclaimed in suitable inscriptions carved in the architrave. The cost of the Peristyle, with its associated buildings, Music Hall and the Casino, was $200,000. The architect was Mr. C. B. Atwood, of Chicago.

SAMOAN GIRLS.—We are accustomed to think of the natives of the South Sea Islands as cannibals, savages; distinguished as much for their fierce appearance as for their cruelty. This illusion was effectually dispelled by the exhibition of Samoans that were a part of the Ethnographic Congress at the World's Fair. The above is a photographic reproduction of a picture taken of two Samoan girls who were seen at the South Sea Island village on the Plaisance. So far from being forbidding in their looks and savage in their natures, the Samoans are among the mildest of people in disposition, and the most comely and symmetrical in form and feature. These girls were seventeen years of age when they came to the Fair, and were conceded to be as splendid specimens of physical womanhood as any country can produce. Their clothing was made entirely of cocoanut fibre, though to appearances their dress was a cotton fabric, and only a careful examination would convince a skeptic that it was not. The Samoans not only make dresses of cocoanut fibre, but they use the leaves of that tree for making a beautifully plaited matting that serves them admirably for carpeting the ground floors of their dwellings. The girls of the coral-begirted islands of the South Pacific are famous swimmers, rivaling their cousins of the Sandwich group, and to this vigorous exercise is due their strength, splendid physique and perfection of form. One of the girls pictured above sat as a model for one of the best artists in New York, who declared he had never before seen a human being so nearly perfect in every physical feature. They are vivacious, charming, and not above the weaknesses of their sex, for they love flattery and flirtation, but morally they are, as a rule, above reproach.

THE COLUMBIAN FOUNTAIN.—A part of the detail of the Columbian Fountain is shown in the above photographic illustration, which fully represents the execution of an exquisite design. To Mr. Frederick MacMonnies belongs the honor of creating such an impressive and strikingly allegoric piece of immense statuary, for which design and completion he received the sum of $50,000. The masterpiece of the Fountain is the Barge of State, with the Genius of Discovery directing the vessel from a lofty seat, upborne by four children of Destiny. Fame as a trumpet herald stands on the prow, and Time controls the helm, while four rowers on each side, typifying Agriculture, Commerce, Industry, Science, Architecture, Music, Painting and Sculpture, propel the ambitious freighted Barge towards the shores of destiny, assisted by four span of sea horses mounted with riders, representing Culture, Intelligence, Heroism and Truth. The Barge occupied the centre of a basin that was one hundred and fifty feet in diameter, which overflowed by cascades at its east face into the lagoon. The playing water was shot up by tritons, mermaids and dolphins that seemed to be sporting in the waves. It was a vision of infinite charm that can never fade from the remembrance of World's Fair visitors.

VIEW FROM SOUTH BASIN, LOOKING NORTH.—Our point of observation, which presents the splendid panorama given in the above picture, is the south veranda of Machinery Hall. In the foreground is shown a corner of the Lion Fountain and pedestal of the Columbian Obelisk, with Potter's Bulls, or Statues of Plenty, facing the lagoon, and in the rear of these is the west façade of the Agricultural Building. The view north comprehends a beautiful vista of lagoon, bridges, statuary and noble structures, that of Manufactures Hall occupying the chief part of the perspective. On the left we have a glimpse of the projecting, columnated front of Machinery Hall, and beyond is a glance of the east side of the Electricity Building. Thence the vision fades into misty outline of the dome of the Illinois Building, and the indistinct, the bare suggestion of structures that line the lagoon on the north, an imitation of a city whose avenues continue their splendor into endless distance.

GENERAL VIEW OF STATE BUILDINGS, NO. 1.—The photograph above shows a part of the north section of the Fair Grounds, and the elevated tracks of the Illinois Central Railroad at Sixtieth Street. We are able to distinguish a number of the State buildings, especially those which are conspicuous by reason of their towers, domes, or other distinguishing architectural features. New York's Building, with its double cupola, and Pennsylvania's, with its high tower imitative of Independence Hall, are easily pointed out, while the lesser buildings appear to be so closely grouped as to require an experienced eye, thoroughly familiar with the appearance of each structure, to individualize and name each one in view. The points of the compass are readily obtained by noting the north end, and the very indistinct outline of the dome of the Art Palace, the more plainly noticeable dome of Illinois Building, and the barely distinguishable roof of Manufactures Hall, far away towards the south.

GENERAL VIEW OF THE STATE BUILDINGS, NO. 2.—The same point of observation serves for a view of the buildings in this picture as that from which the photograph printed on the opposite side was taken. In the above is shown the pond upon which the Esquimaux were encamped, south of which we see the graceful crown of California's Building, conforming to the style of an old Mission. Twenty other State buildings are more plainly shown, with the capitoline dome of Illinois Building commanding the chief view, the centre from which a majority of the State structures radiated. Beyond it, in the hazy distance, is discerned the peak of the Administration Building, and to the left, but in almost complete obscurity, is the faint shadow of the Obelisk, which terminates the south basin between Machinery and Agricultural Halls. But though the view is an indistinct one, because of the close grouping of buildings, it is singularly beautiful, and strikingly impressive for the magnificence which it outlines.

THE PROMENADE AND GAS TORCHES ON ADMINISTRATION BUILDING.—All the beauties and advantages of Administration Building were not discoverable by a view from the Fair Grounds, nor yet by an inspection of the interior, for a visit to any of its galleries was repaid by the finding of some unexpected novelty of grandeur and advantage, exhibiting an infinitude of detail in the design, ornamentation and adaptation of the structure. The photograph here presented shows the promenade that circled the building at the base of the dome, also the splendid gas torches, twelve feet high, and one of Karl Better's groups representing the Victories of Science and the Achievements of Peace. The elevation was sufficient to afford an expansive view of the entire grounds, and that too from the centre of the finest buildings and most extravagant sculptuary decorations of the Fair. Unhappily, an accident to one of the Victory Group prompted the authorities to close the stairway leading to the promenade, except to those holding special permits, for which reason comparatively few persons had the pleasure of sweeping the grounds from this lofty vantage point.

A DROMEDARY OF THE STEPPES.—A typical Bedouin, with his main transportation dependence, stands before us in the photograph, nothing being omitted in the characterization of the roving bandit of the Asiatic Steppes, as he is seen in his own desert country. His tarboosh, bournouse and gibbeh, his trusty scimeter, and a countenance reflective of the cruel instinct that he vainly seeks to hide beneath his richly colored robes, are conspicuous as they are typical. His patient beast of burden, demure, but equally treacherous, and as wondrously bedizened with finely embroidered trappings as his master, appears to be conscious of the prominence he has assumed in the public's estimation, and in the photographer's eye, for no one ever affected a lordlier air when having his picture taken than does this beast of many virtues and more numerous faults. Riding a camel is more hazardous to the untrained than a trip on the switchback, but not nearly so exciting, for which reason, possibly, as American natures are contraries, half the World's Fair visitors entertained an ambition to go camel riding, while a very big proportion of them gratified their desire, at an expense of a quarter each.

EAST INDIA JUGGLERS.—Much has been written about the astounding feats of juggling performed by the fakirs of India, who it has been repeatedly declared, suffer themselves to be buried alive for months, who thrust knives through their bodies, who climb heavenward by means of a rope thrown towards the sky and suspended by invisible means. People have read these accounts so frequently that a great many believe them, and for this reason Indian jugglers were brought to the Fair ostensibly to perform their legerdemain, but primarily to delude the sophisticated. They gave their exhibitions in a hut on the north side of the Plaisance, and were liberally patronized; but no reward was great enough to induce them to exhibit the amazing powers with which Munchausen travelers credited them. Those at the Fair were no doubt as skillful as their brother artists, but their performances were limited to such tricks as every American boy has seen a hundred times, and which many a boy can duplicate. Tales of travelers, like those of amateur fishermen, are not easily verified, and it is well to doubt the ability of India jugglers to perform those magical feats which many have heard of but which in fact no one has ever seen.

MAMMALIA EXHIBIT OF SMITHSONIAN INSTITUTE.—There was no display in any of the main buildings that attracted greater interest than the Smithsonian Institute exhibits, which occupied several sections in the Government Building. Many branches of natural science were represented, and that of natural history was especially complete with North American specimens, and some from foreign lands. In preparing the collection of mammalia exhibited at the Fair, a large corps of skilled workmen were employed for a period of two years, under the direction of William Palmer, taxidermist of the Institute, and the specimens, gathered from every part of our domain, were mounted in a manner to counterfeit life, so that, save to the critical inspector, the animals looked as if they were contemplating their surroundings. The photographic view herewith shows only a small part of the Mammalia Exhibit, but gives an excellent idea of the character of the display, which is nowhere equaled except in the British Museum.

AUSTRIA'S FINE ART DISPLAY.—Joining Germany's exhibit on the north, along Columbia Avenue in Manufactures Building, was Austria's superb display, which was opened for inspection as early as May 3. Glassware predominated in the front part of the section, in which were shown the finest specimens of Bohemian production, in a profusion of rich coloring. In the centre of the display was a huge onyx vase, belonging to Emperor Francis Joseph, girdled with exquisitely carved groups and chaste figures. Another specially beautiful thing in the display, was a huge punch bowl with glasses to match, gilded inside and chased with a complicated arabesque vine pattern on the outside, while each had a handle that represented a dragon. There were other delicate pieces of glassware, pottery and ivory, and a set of Pompeiian red ware of six pieces that was valued at $8000, which was only exceeded in value by two urns six feet in height, set on pedestals, and hand-painted at Carlsbad by the greatest artist of that city. There were a thousand things of infinite charm and almost indescribable magnificence in the Austrian fine arts display, of which we are able to give only a picture of the façade and portal.

ENTRANCE TO THE GERMAN VILLAGE.—Near the north centre of the Midway was the German Castle and Village, a curious reminder of feudal times that seemed to bear upon its walls the mould of many centuries. The entrance was by way of a drawbridge crossing a moat, through an arched gate-way protected by a portcullis, and thence into a spacious hall, upon the walls of which were hung mediæval armor, bows and ancient weapons. From the hall was an entrance that led to a museum, where there was a display of antiquities appertaining to the age of chivalry. The village proper, which covered three or four acres of space, consisted of reproductions of very old German habitations, with small porticos and sharp gables, built around a court, in the centre of which was a music stand. This open space, corresponding somewhat to a village green, was the wine and beer garden, and under a roofed but open-sided annex was a German restaurant, where dishes peculiar to that country were served. A band of twenty musicians, in white uniforms and military caps, gave hourly concerts, which were so enjoyable, that large crowds of visitors were in constant attendance.

LITTLE BI-LO OF THE LAPLAND VILLAGE.—Babies of strange peoples have a fascination for us greater even than have the customs which often excite our amazement. Indian mothers have always found large profit in exhibiting their papooses to overland travelers, and who is it that would not give a quarter for a peep at a real Chinese baby? It was this curiosity that lead thousands of persons to visit the Lapland Village on the Plaisance, where it was well advertised there was a wee little native tot called Bi-Lo, to be seen. Our picture shows this attractive bit of Lapland infancy lying in a sledge at the edge of one of the two turf huts, apparently very happy, but in fact evidently very warm, for it was a hot day when the photograph was taken, and little Bi-Lo is in winter dress. The tight fitting leg wear may be taken by some as a suggestion of male sex, but Bi-Lo was a girl, robust, roguish and frolicsome among her people, but exhibited shyness when approached by strangers. Her feet are covered with bear-skin moccasins, and she is resting on a large skin of the same animal, though bears are not so common as wolves in Lapland. The canoe-like sledge was brought from that country to illustrate the kind of conveyance which the Laps use, and was drawn about the village enclosure by a reindeer, whose harness is shown in the picture.

REPRODUCTION OF A STREET IN OLD VIENNA.—Many persons who attended the Fair came away with the impression that the most interesting exhibit of old time things was the Street Scene in Vienna, representing that city as it appeared four hundred years ago or at the time America was discovered. The impression produced upon the visitor was peculiar, for every detail of the reproduction was so unique as to create a feeling in each visitor that he was not only actually in contact with, but was a part of the life of long, long ago. Painters had done their work well in making the street perspective a lengthy one, along both sides of which were steep-gabled and tiled-roofed houses, with latticed windows and pretty little balconies hardly large enough for an eloping couple. The street was narrow, after the character which distinguished nearly all cities centuries ago, and were fairly choked with pedestrians; bazaar after bazaar lined the way, where all imaginable wares were exposed for sale by men and women dressed in costumes which prevailed four hundred years ago. In the court, or Volksgarten, was a music pavilion, where the Austrian band gave concerts daily at two-hour intervals. About this court seats were placed, and also wine tables, where people were served with wine and beer by gretchens who looked quaint in their antique garb of red skirts, white aprons, black bodices and wooden-soled slippers, but who were, in fact, as entertaining as modern bar-maids, and were equally urgent in soliciting custom. The illusion of an ancient city was further increased by a Quaker wall, which separated the exhibition from the Plaisance, and which was crenelated and towered after the manner of cities of the period represented.

THE COLUMBIAN CARAVELS.—On the south side of the long pier, near the Convent of La Rabida, lay moored a reproduction of the three vessels in which Columbus made his first great voyage westward. The *Santa Maria* was built by the Spanish Government and presented to this nation, while the *Nina* and *Pinta* were likewise constructed in Spain, but at the expense of the United States. Each one of the three vessels was an exact counterpart, both in size and detail, of its original, the reproduction being carried even to the equipment and armament, and all were manned by Spanish sailors, who brought them safely across the Atlantic over the same route that Columbus pursued, though they were accompanied by a United States and a Spanish man-of-war. The *Santa Maria* had a covered deck, but the *Nina* and *Pinta* were open caravels, fifty-four feet long and eight feet depth of hold. Those who examined these diminutive crafts, and are familiar with the mammoth ocean-going steamers of to-day, were moved to greater wonder than they ever felt before how Columbus contrived to survive the stormy perils to which he was subjected on his first return voyage.

ETHNOLOGICAL GALLERY, SMITHSONIAN INSTITUTE.—In the Government Building the Smithsonian Institute made an exhibit so complete in every department of Natural Science that it would have required a week's time to examine all the specimens shown. The photograph above presents a beautiful view of the gallery devoted to the Ethnographic display. The busts seen on pedestals in the foreground are of famous Indian chiefs, and the full figures noticed in the glass cases represent types of North American Indians. The exhibit in this gallery was largely confined to native tribes, not only to representing the appearance of the people, but likewise to illustrating the traits and characteristics of each tribe. Accordingly, there were figures in appropriate costumes, and in positions that indicated action, illustrative of labor, hunting, traveling and domesticity, while there was a very large display of the products of handiwork wrought by men and women of the various North American tribes, such as dressed skins, lace work, beaded articles, models of canoes, weapons, moccasins, feather work, scalplocks fantastically arranged, hair work, and numerous other specimens that exhibited great skill and patient application.

THE FISHERIES BUILDING.—The exhibit of fresh and sea water creatures was made in what was called the Fisheries Building, whose extreme dimensions were 200 x 1100 feet, with two circular annexes 135 feet in diameter. The exterior of the structure was Spanish Romanesque, the walls a dull brown stone color, and the roof was red Spanish tile, the different shades harmonizing beautifully. The building was subdivided into three parts and in each was a distinct exhibit. The central portion was devoted to general fisheries, the north section contained the angling exhibit, and in the south division were the aquaria. This latter was reached through a tunnel way, along the sides of which were continuous tanks alive with fresh water fish. The feature of the middle section was a circular pond with a large fountain in the centre throwing up a heavy stream of water and a myriad of fish swimming in the basin. The length of the glass fronts of the aquaria was 575 feet, and the tanks ranged in capacity from 750 to 1500 gallons. The fresh water exhibit contained nearly every known American species of fish, while the marine display was almost equally complete, excepting only the very large creatures. The supply of sea water was obtained by evaporating the necessary quantity at the Wood Hall Station of the U. S. Fish Commission.

PICTURE OF THE GREELEY EXPEDITION.—In the rotunda of the Government Building, near the quartermaster's section, was a large model in plaster of a realistic Arctic scene, with its bleak desolation of tumultous ice-packs and boundless fields of snow glaring under a sun that dazzles but does not heat. The scene depicted by the model represents General Greeley welcoming back and congratulating Lieutenant Lockwood and Sergeant Brainard after their return, in 1882, from latitude 83° 24' north, the nearest approach to the north pole ever made by Arctic explorers. It was a beautiful combination of model and painting, that exhibited such an excellent reproduction of this memorable incident, that it drew immense crowds, who thronged in front of it almost continually, and whose interest and admiration was unbounded. A brief history of the event, and Greeley's expedition, was recorded in the two bulletins shown in the illustration.

THE STATUE OF PLENTY.—On a staff pedestal on the south side of the Grand Basin, near the Casino, was Potter's heroic Statue of Plenty, a strong double-figure representing the Cerean Goddess standing beside the Bull of Strength with a stalk of corn in her right hand. Though a departure from the common allegoric figure of Ceres pouring the fruits of husbandry from the Horn of Plenty, the significance of Potter's statue was equally apparent, and for his originality in the treatment of the subject, art connoisseurs have bestowed upon him the most generous applause. The statue occupied a conspicuous position, commanding the south turn of the main basin at the water-approach to the Peristyle, by which the electric launches and gondolas carried their passengers, and paused to give opportunity for its inspection. The view at this point was the most charming that was presented within the Fair area, as it commanded the full length of the basin and the magnificent buildings that bordered it, together with the finest pieces of statuary that adorned the vantage places in the central section of the grounds.

ON THE ROOF OF MANUFACTURES BUILDING.—What a glorious panorama was unfolded from the lofty promenade that extended around the roof of Manufactures Building! Two hundred feet from the earth, nearly as high as Bunker Hill Monument, away up where birds of tireless wing take their exercises, the view comprehended a boundless scope of lake and prairie, while below, in marvelous distinctness, lay the architectural splendors and peerless grandeurs of the World-involving Exposition. Beside the persons on the roof balcony, as shown in the photograph, is the great search-light reflector, whose beams of light were so fierce that they penetrated the darkness like a meteor, and flashed their sky-piercing rays so high and luminous that people nearly one hundred miles away could see the reflection. These mammoth search lights were used most effectively in increasing the beauties of the night illuminations of the Electric Fountains and Administration Building, but they are now used by the Government at dangerous points along the Atlantic Coast to give warnings to vessels.

STREET CARRIERS OF CONSTANTINOPLE.—The photograph herewith pictures a section of the Transportation Building, and is illustrative of the Street Carriers of Constantinople. Donkeys are favorite beasts of burden in the cities of European Turkey, so we observe most conspicuous in the picture one of the little animals dressed in a packsaddle as if waiting with great patience for his load. Other figures represent men drawing carts, trundling two-wheeled barrows, and carrying heavy trays upon their heads. On the farther side of the donkey is a complete model of one of the palatial steamers belonging to the Fall River Line, and in the foreground, lying upon the floor, is a Turkish riding-saddle, such as is used by the common people of European Turkey.

APPROACH AND PORTICO OF THE TRANSPORTATION BUILDING.—The golden, or more properly the silvern, doorway to the Transportation Building constituted a feature so rich, symmetrical, and altogether beautiful, that passing crowds paused before it with bewildered admiration, but there were associated architectural features which commanded only secondary interest. There was a side approach by a winding way to an oriental portico, the treatment of which was so unique and charming as to fairly divide honors with the splendid doorway. There was an air of Byzantian elegance, of delicious dreamy and delightful repose suggested by the exquisite nook that seemed to invite indulgence in tea and the sweet vision-creating chibouk, the soul of Turkish contentfulness. The solid balustrade that ran around the tasteful veranda was richly decorated with relief patterns, and vignettes of beautiful designs, while an allegoric cartoon, representing ancient modes of transportation, embellished the facing below the veranda. The effect was remarkably pleasing.

THE GERMAN FOUNTAIN.—Germany's Building had a lake front location between that of Great Britain and Spain, extending 150 x 175 feet, and was one of the grandest structures on the grounds. While the main front was east, facing the lake, the building really "stood four square to the winds," and on the west front was a splendid wood, which was beautified by German workmen until it possessed attractions in keeping with the magnificent building it partially enclosed. The most beautiful feature of the wooded grounds was the handsome fountain shown in the photograph, the work of Martin and Piltzing, Berlin. It was a reproduction of one which stands in the palace grounds at Berlin, and while of less costly material, was to the sight as picturesque as the original. The height of this composition fountain was twenty-five feet, surmounted by an electric globe, symbolizing the light of knowledge. Near the basin were also statues of deer and dogs, to add animation to the forest scene, an effect which, however, was destroyed by signs reading, "Keep off the Grass."

BRAZILIAN EXHIBIT IN MINES AND MINING BUILDING.—Sandwiched between the mineral displays of Idaho and California was the splendid exhibit made by Brazil, which included a large showing of such products as phosphates, gold, silver and diamonds. The piece d'resistance of her display was, however, a sharp cone standing on an open pedestal and mounting its summit fifteen feet high, looking like a gigantic pyramid of pure gold. The base was eight feet square, and this conical block represented the amount of gold that has been extracted from the mines of a single State in Brazil between the years 1720 and 1820. The weight and value of this precious product may be plainly read on the pyramid shown so clearly in the photograph. The pyramid was made of staff and covered with gold-leaf, in admirable simulation of the tremendous cone of gold it represented.

LIMOGES CATHEDRAL GALLERY.—In the south court, in the French section of Sculptures, was the most pretentious example of antique and elaborate carving that was shown at the Fair. It was a representation of the gallery in the Cathedral of Limoges, a Sixteenth Century work of art by an unknown sculptor. It is strange that the name of the wonderful workman should be in eternal eclipse, while that of Jean de Langeac, the Bishop of Limoges, should be preserved to fame through no other merit than that of having ordered the sculptor to produce this remarkable gallery. Description can add little to the attractive beauty of the gallery as exhibited in the photograph. And almost equally beautiful are the chaste statuary groups of defenders of the faith and angels around and on the tomb of Lamoriciere, a superb and grand work by the chisel of Ludovic Durand. On the right is a life-size marble by Hugues, representing "Immortality," an old man in a boat being drawn over the River of Life by a winged child.

U. S. BATTLESHIP ILLINOIS.—The efficiency of the United States Navy was illustrated at the Fair by a model battleship constructed upon piling beside a pier at which boats from the city discharged their passengers who, after leaving the landing, went directly through the Government Plaza. This model ship, which was in fact a fac-simile of the powerful 10,300-ton coast-line battleship "Illinois," appeared to be at her anchorage, but was in fact a superstructure resting on heavy piling which rose to within five feet of the water-line. Her largest guns were wood models, but quite a number were heavy ordnance pieces capable of terrible execution. The ship was complete in every department, from sleeping quarters to gun-deck, and besides these she was steel armor-plated below the berth-deck, and above decks were steel turrets and redoubts, through portholes of which projected deep-mouthed 8-inch and 13-inch wood guns. The total length of the Illinois was 248 feet, and her beam was 65 feet 3 inches. She was fully manned and officered with a crew of 200 men, who gave daily drills, and in everything performed the duties required of them when in actual service on the high seas.

UNITED STATES STATUARY EXHIBIT.—Continuing through the north court of the Art Building the scene as above photographed catches our eye, in which the following splendid pieces of sculpture are displayed: The relief marble in the foreground is Caroline Brooks' figure of "The Dreaming Iolanthe," and the standing nude marble is by the same sculptress, whose subject is "Lady Godiva." The gigantic centre piece is a bronze by Ball, of Washington, and the bronze equestrian statue of Paul Revere, on the extreme right, is also by Ball. On the left are marbles, one representing "Diana and the Lion," or intellect dominating brute force, is by Elwell; and another, "Christ and the Little Child," is by Ball. The heroic statue of Washington, while a fine piece of work, showed to such poor advantage that many persons, knowing nothing of art, turned away with expressions of disgust. This was, of course, due to the close view which they had. The statue was borrowed from Boston, where it occupies an elevation sufficiently high to show the features perfectly, and thus viewed it is one of the best figures ever produced of our country's father.

UNITED STATES EXHIBIT OF SCULPTURE.—The scene here photographed is a section of the north court, just outside the rotunda of Art Hall. The main group on the right is a large bronze group of Charles Dickens and Little Nell, a superb work of art by Elwell. The second large figures are of plaster, by Bush-Brown, and represent a Buffalo Hunt. Far in the rear is seen a part of Searles' heroic bronze statue of Washington. On the extreme left is a magnificent plaster of Lincoln, a specimen of Rogers' statuary. Between Lincoln and the Buffalo Hunt is a life-size bronze group by Clark, entitled "The Cider Press," a very striking piece intended for a fountain. All the figures on this section were strong in treatment rather than idealistic.

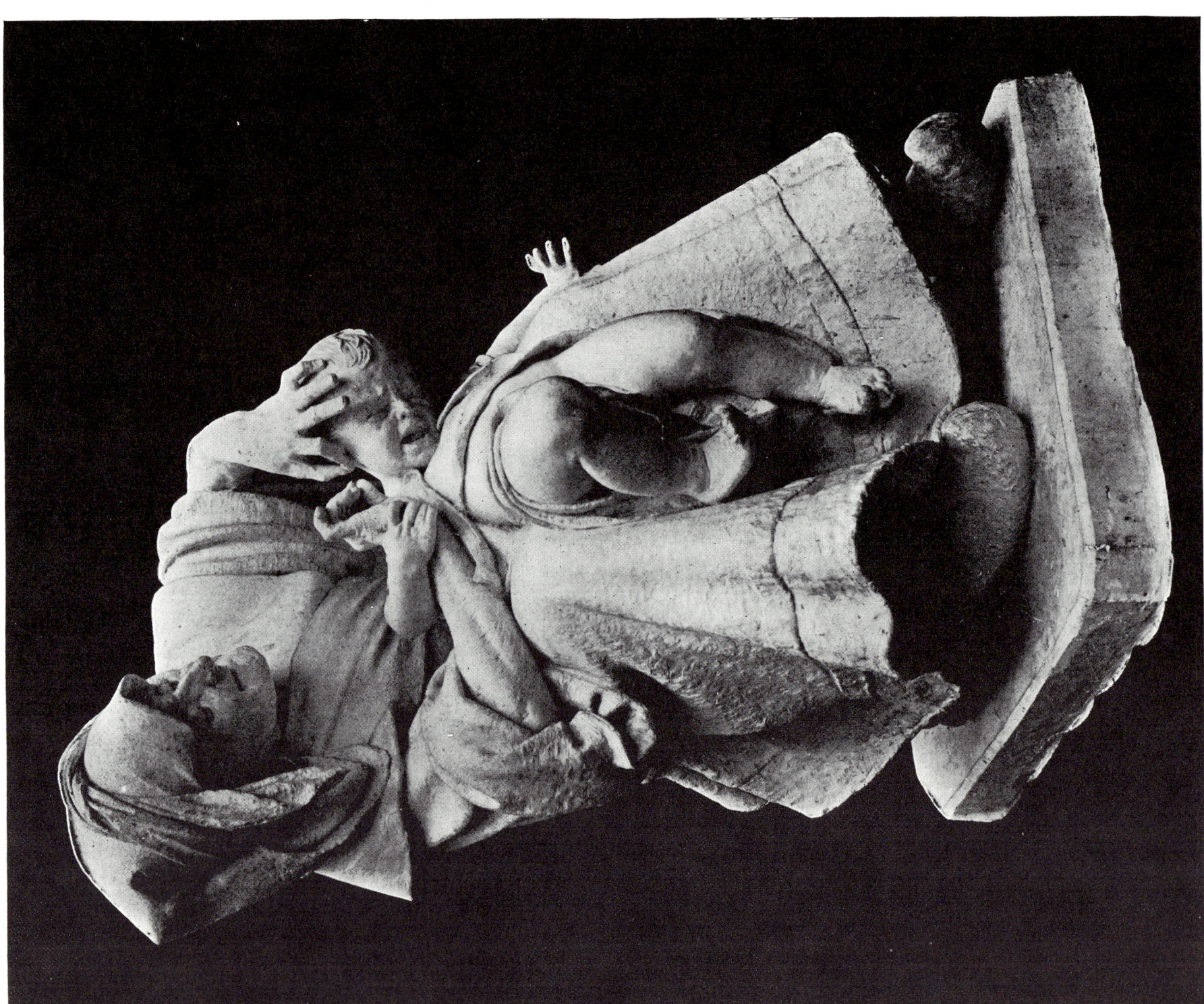

THE FIRST PAIR OF EARRINGS.—In the Spanish section, which was located in the west court of Fine Arts Hall, was a very delightful character plaster entitled "The First Pair of Earrings." In one catalogue the piece is credited to C. Folgueras, and in another to Miguel Angel Trellez, an illustration of the evil effects of keeping the title and artist's name off figures and paintings, in order that publishers of art catalogues may thrive. The figure is that of a grandmother touching a very young child with the first sting of vanity, and the sculptor has been so faithful in his execution, as well as natural in his conception, that the work is readily recognized as a masterpiece. In the child's face and contortions we discern a mingling of fright and agony, while the expression given to the wooden-shoed and heavy-kirtled old lady is that of sympathetic resolution that tells her thoughts, "You will bless me for it hereafter."

SHIPWRECKED.—Spanish sculptors, as well as painters, contributed largely of their work towards making the Art display at the Exposition a memorable success. In the west court of the Art Building was the display of Spanish Statuary, of which the photograph above was a prominent example. The group was a plaster by M. Frilles, a French name, but probably a resident of Spain. The subject treated is "Shipwrecked," but while the figures are good they do not fully express the idea of the artist. The base was too small for natural treatment, and the unclothed figures clinging to a piece of broken mast apparently set firmly upright in the earth leads to confusion, and a majority of persons who saw the group believed that it represented the Stone Age, though they could not understand the rope and iron ring. The figures are evidently that of son and father, the former half drowned and lashed to a mast, while the father is crying out against the storm for help as he drifts almost hopelessly on the fatal waves.

A JAVANESE DWELLING.—A very excellent idea is obtained of the style and character of Javanese houses by an examination of the accompanying photograph. The village was a perfect copy of those which may be seen along the southwest coast of Java, as it was built by native carpenters from imported material. There is a slight departure from original custom in the doors to the dwelling, characteristic of the imitative instinct of all people when brought into strange association. Among the common people it is the custom to make no provision against thieves, their houses being as a rule without doors. But dishonesty is almost unknown among the Javanese outside of the larger cities; in these, however, mixture with foreign races has had the inevitable result of debasing the natives. There is little or no temptation to thieves in the small villages or rural homes, because the Javanese rarely have any valuable belongings, and those fortunate enough to acquire money never leave it about the house, which is liable at any moment to be swept away by fire, as all their buildings are of very inflammable material.

GOVERNMENT ARMY EXHIBIT.—In the southeast part of the Government Building, between the Ordnance and Engineer sections, were departments containing exhibits of gun and cartridge making machines, metal works, and of campaign materials and battle-flags. The section shown in the photograph was one of particular interest, since in it was displayed the greatest collection of historic battle-flags that was ever seen outside of a Government Museum. Besides these remarkable mementoes of all the wars that have disturbed the country since the Jamestown settlement, there were garrison equipage, packsaddles, mountain howitzers mounted on mules, propellor torpedoes, forage wagons, and every imaginable kind of camp paraphernalia There were also many famous relics, such as a beautifully carved bronze cannon, that was captured from the British at Yorktown in 1781; the great gun called "Long Tom," with which the privateer, "General Armstrong," repulsed a British squadron off the Azores in 1814; an ambulance wagon that went through the long campaign of the Potomac, and many other carefully preserved souvenirs of American history.

No. 1.—A PART OF THE FRENCH SCULPTURE EXHIBIT.—In the south court of the Art Building was a remarkably beautiful display of French sculpture work, in which, of course, the nude predominated. The figures most prominent in the illustration are as follows: in the foreground is the marble relief elsewhere noticed of "The Dreaming Iolanthe." The central heroic group represents the "Republic of France," by the famous sculptor Falguiere, who made it upon the order of his government. The bronze dog in front is "Fox, a pointer," by Fougues. In the rear is a bronze group of an eagle and vulture fighting over the carcass of a bear, by the sculptor Cain. On the extreme left is a plaster of "Diana Reclining," by Warner, and near it is "Ariadne Abandoned," in marble, by Aire, and a bronze group by Turner of "The Herald of Peace." Some of the pieces in the rear are better shown in the companion photograph in this number.

No. 2.—A PART OF THE FRENCH SCULPTURE EXHIBIT.—One of the very striking animal groups in the department of sculpture, remarkable for its realism as well as for size, is Cain's plaster representing a rhinoceros attacked by tigers. The attitudes are very incarnations of ferocity, before which the timid irresistibly shrank from a sudden approach. In the background is again seen imperfectly the Republic of France statue, and in front of that is a bewitching figure of Diana lifting her bow above her head as if signaling to her companion huntresses. It is by Falguiere, and is one of his greatest creations. On the extreme right, barely glimpsed between two pillars, are the life-size figures of Washington and Lafayette in plaster, by Bartholdi.

A SECTION OF THE UNITED STATES EXHIBIT OF OIL PAINTINGS.—The room shown in the above photograph was in Department K of the exhibit of American paintings, and shows the arrangement of the pictures and means of lighting better than it does the pictures. The principal and largest painting in the photograph was entitled "The Returning Flock," a beautiful pastoral scene by Ben. Foster, of New York. The picture at the top of the left-hand corner was "The Flower Maker," by Harriet Foss, while the top picture adjoining was "The First Days of Spring," also one of Foster's idyllic creations. The other paintings are too indistinct to justify particular description, but the artists represented in the room, besides the two mentioned, were Miss Gertrude, of Philadelphia; Mary Fowler, of New York; Frank Fowler, of the same city; Miss Fairchild, of Boston; W. Forsyth, of Indianapolis; and several others whose work was equally creditable, but whose names are not yet so well known in the art world.

CHRIST AND THE ADULTERESS.—The great South American Republic, famous for its insurrections and other political disturbances, is likewise renowned for its devotion to Catholicism and religious observance. Some of the most beautiful specimens of human energy and artistic handiwork that were seen at the Fair, were also products of Brazilian workmen, illustrating the progress that country is making in manufactures and creative arts. The most exquisite example of the latter was Professor Bernardelli's marble group representing "Christ and the Adulteress," which was placed in the Brazilian section of the Art Hall. The divine figure, even in cold marble, seems warm with sympathy, so singularly life-like is the pose that speaks upbraidingly to the mob, "He that is without sin, let him cast the first stone." There is compassion and rebuke in the Saviour's face; there is self-abasement and mortification in the figure of the crouching woman. No other marble in the Art Building conveyed a lesson so strong, that appealed to the heart so speakingly, as that of "Christ and the Adulteress."

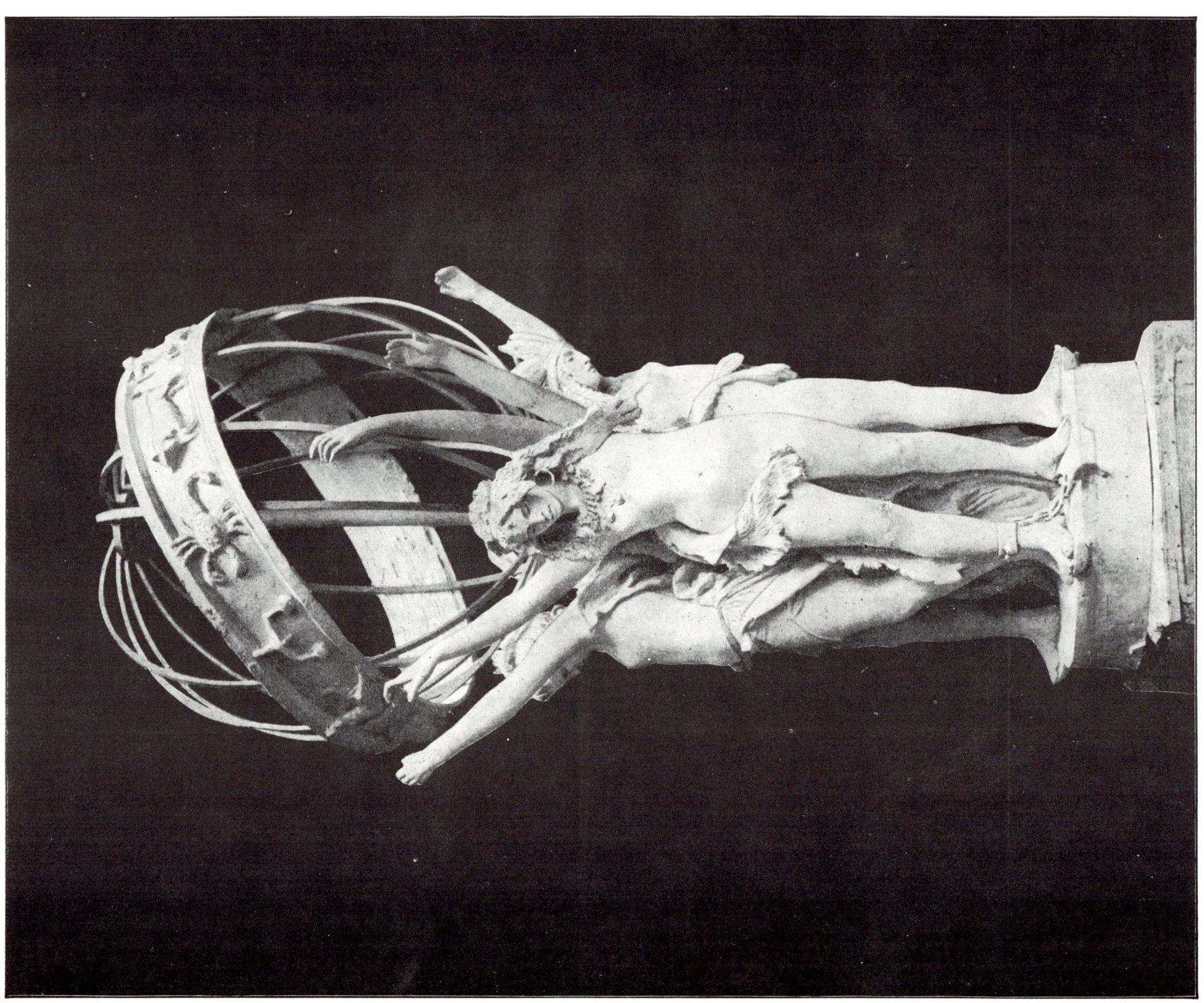

MARTINY'S SCULPTURES ON AGRICULTURAL HALL.—Some of the finest sculpture work that was to be seen at the Exposition adorned Agricultural Hall, the second largest building on the grounds. Chief among these beautiful creations of art were the four typical groups that stood upon the corners of that great structure. Each of these groups was composed of four nude figures, representing the four great races of civilization, supporting a globe of longitudinal lines, bound by an equatorial belt, on which were the signs of the zodiac. The same idea was expressed in the sculpture work of Trocadero Fountain in Paris, but the figures seen there were neither so classical nor so symmetrical as those above pictured from the Agricultural Building groups.

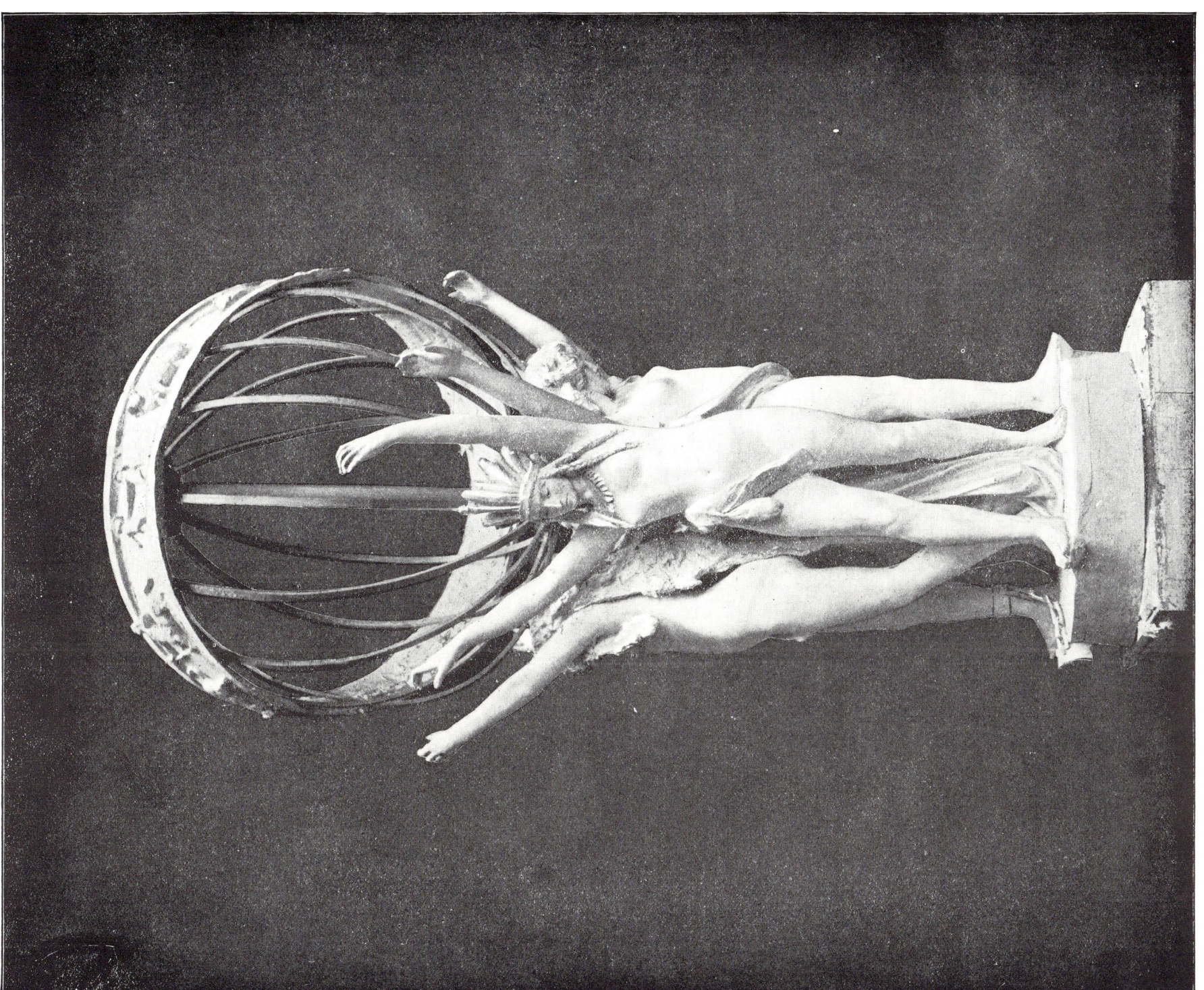

ANOTHER GROUP OF MARTINY'S HOROSCOPE.—The picture here presented, exhibits another view of the statuary groups that stood upon the corners of Agricultural Hall, as more particularly described under the picture on the opposite page. The four figures represent not only the four great races, but also the four corners of the world, whose civilization they typify and support. The chaste figure in front stands as the American type, an Indian girl whose form is divinely fair, decidedly idealistic, but flattering to American pride, for though pretty Indian maidens are seldom or never really seen, they are very common in the story books.

A ROOM IN THE NEW ENGLAND CABIN.—It was a happy idea that occurred to Emma S. Britton, the construction of an olden-time New England cabin, wherein everything should be a faithful reproduction of the manners, style and characteristics of the colonial fathers and mothers. She obtained a concession and erected her ideal cabin on the Plaisance, and till the close of the Fair served New England dinners, with handsome young Puritan ladies in colonial costumes as waitresses. One portion of the double cabin was used as a restaurant, and the other as a living room for ye olden family, of which our photograph is a splendid picture. In this department, ladies in the dress of our foremothers rocked the canoe cradle, knit yarn socks, carded wool, spun yarn, drank from gourds, and gossiped like Priscilla about their John Aldens and other likely fellows, who were at meeting last Sunday, or attended singing school. The cabin was a great curiosity that attracted much attention, especially from old people.

THE KRUPP BUILDING.—On the lake front, south of the Convent of La Rabida, was the Krupp Building, towered at the ends after a style common in Germany for several centuries, and emblazoned with the German coat of arms. Within this strong structure was a wondrous display of gigantic weaponry manufactured at Friedrich Krupp's monster iron works in Essen. Along the west wall were sixteen enormous cannons mounted ready for action, with shot and shells lying to hand beside them. In the centre of this group of deadly enginery was the largest gun ever cast, whose weight is 122½ tons, and which throws a 1200 pound steel pointed projectile a distance of fifteen miles. It takes 600 pounds of powder at each full discharge and the cost of firing it is $1000. On the east side of the building were castings and steel armor plates, showing rudders, shafts, screws, and other parts of modern steamers, and steel beaks for ramming vessels. A fine wrought-iron balcony, executed by Dusseldorf workmen, extended around the building, from which a splendid view of the exhibits could be had.

THE WORK OF SCULPTURING THE BIG FIGURES.—It was an interesting sight to watch the work of forming the heroic staff figures with which the buildings and grounds were generously ornamented. The first step was the making of a working model by the chief sculptor. This being done a frame of wood and iron was made, upon which the staff material was applied until a big chunk of shapeless staff was formed. This was therefore the block from which were carved the figures. The work of fashioning the figures was not done by specially skillful sculptors, until the last touches of the master-hand were needed to impart the perfect likeness of the ideal as represented in the model. The photograph above shows some of the workmen with tools in hand, and a group of statuary that was about ready to be lifted into position on the Administration Building.

A BEAUTIFUL DISPLAY OF CHURCH FURNITURE.—The above photograph pictures a portion of the exhibit made in Manufactures Hall by Hems & Sons, of England. This magnificent exhibition of carved church furniture was one of the sights of the exhibition toward which devout visitors turned again and again, especially to study the holy figures carved with wonderful skill to life-like representation. On the extreme left is a glimpse of Harrison & Sons display of gorgeous glazes and enamels.

NORTHEAST VIEW FROM MANUFACTURES BUILDING.—A splendid panorama is presented in the above photograph, the view being taken from the roof of Manufactures Building looking northeast and lakeward. The dome of the Government Building is a prominent feature of the view, and east of it is seen the Government Plaza and the pretty tents of the Life Saving Corps. Thence further east is the lake shore promenade, and clearly distinguishable are the white sides and dark upper works of the Battle Ship at her mooring, beside the north pier boat landing. The isolated house near the Battle Ship is Great Britain's Building, and west of this are the government buildings of Spain and Germany, while the never finished Spectatorium looms up hazily just outside the north boundary of the Fair grounds. Other structures discernible dimly are the Fisheries Building, Swedish Building, and Art Palace, and lakeward the view expires in a stretch of distance to where the horizon drops down upon the blue water.

THE OLD CONVENT OF LA RABIDA.—One of the sacredly regarded objects to which all World's Fair visitors made a pious pilgrimage, was a *fac simile* reproduction of the old Convent of La Rabida, famous for all future ages as the holy place where Columbus found shelter in the hour of his greatest need, and where his plans of discovery received the weighty encouragement and aid of good father Perez. The reproduced convent was set upon a promontory in imitation of the original that overlooks Palos and the sea, and all about were planted such vegetation as clings to the sterile soil around La Rabida. But inside were the greater things of interest, for the Pope, Duke of Veragua the lineal descendant of Columbus, the Spanish Government, and the West Indies lent all their Columbian relics, which made a collection of pictures, manuscripts, weapons, money, and memorials that fairly filled several rooms. Upon everything wore the stamp, the air, the remembrance of feudal times, the age of chivalry, and the achievements of Columbus. Cost of the building was $50,000.

THE CALIFORNIA STATUE.—California made herself famous at the Fair by erecting a State Building next in size to that of Illinois, and by making the largest fruit display that was to be seen on the grounds. The interior of the California Building was so lofty that it permitted of the constructing of a long gallery, which served not only as additional space for exhibits, but afforded a charming promenade from which a survey of all the many wonders that made up the display could be perfectly viewed. One of the prettiest objects to be seen amid so great a profusion of beautiful and interesting things, was the California Statue, shown in our photograph, which was advantageously positioned next to the exhibit of farm products from Humboldt County. The figure typifies the vintage, fruits and cereals from which the State derives its wealth. The statue also represents Columbia, clothed with the national flag and holding in her left hand a Columbian shield and banner, as a sign of California's patriotism and loyalty to the Union.

FIRST LOCOMOTIVE EVER BROUGHT TO CHICAGO.—Under the sheds of Transportation Building, on the west side of the main structure, were exhibits of primitive railroads of such curious character as to excite greater interest than the displays of luxurious coaches and colossal locomotives. Here was to be seen a section of the first railroad ever laid, with rails of wood fastened to blocks of stone, over which a truck-car was drawn by a horse. There was also a section of the first iron railroad, and the original Stevenson engine, called the "Rocket," the first locomotive ever built, that ran between Liverpool and Manchester in 1826. Though not nearly so old as some other locomotives exhibited at the Fair, the first engine ever brought to Chicago aroused as much curiosity. It is shown in the above photograph, and did service on the road between Chicago and Milwaukee in 1850. It is not so long ago, but since that time Chicago has grown from a trading post to be the second city in America.

GREAT BRITAIN'S FISHERIES EXHIBIT.—Upon entering the west door of the Fisheries Building, the first exhibit on the right was that of Great Britain, consisting chiefly of fishing-tackle, nets, seines lines, etc., and a model of an Irish fishing-school. There were also relief plaster casts of all English fishes, natural in size and coloring, and handsomely arranged, as shown in the above photograph. On the left of the picture is seen a part of the United States' display of small fishing boats, fish-hooks, nets, and other necessary accessories of the successful fishermen, including everything except bait, and even this was represented artificially.

DISPLAY OF SCULPTURE IN THE ITALIAN SECTION.—Our photograph here gives a view of one-half of the Italian Statuary section in the Art Building; also portions of the architectural exhibits made by American architects in the galleries. The central piece is a design for a public building, in which American and Italian styles are harmoniously blended. The figure best distinguished is a marble statue, by Ferrari, representing "The Death of Lincoln." Other pieces shown in the photograph include a bronze by Ximenes, entitled "Caught," the subject being an eagle who, while pilfering, has stepped into a steel trap; "The Last of the Spartans," a marble statue by Trentanove; "Night," a marble medallion, in relief, by Dausch; "The Love Letter," a marble statue, by Gonnella; "A Sea Nymph," by Bardi; and an exquisite statuette of a "Bacchanti," by Soeboeck.

WOODED ISLAND AND THE FISHERIES BUILDING.—One of the most romantic and picturesque spots imaginable was Wooded Island, that might have been a chosen place for Flora and the butterflies, as it was abloom with flowers and sweet shrubberies. The island is admirably pictured in the above photograph, showing a section of its beauties, and the great Fisheries Building on the opposite side of the lagoon. On this island was to be seen the most extensive and magnificent collection of rhododendrons and chrysanthemums that was ever made, while the exhibition of other kinds of flowers, plants and shrubbery was scarcely less complete. The portion of the island shown in the photograph was park-like, and inviting to those who sought a promenade over pretty walks, that were lined with charming flower-beds formed into charming designs aflame with color.

CHINESE THEATRE AND JOSS HOUSE.—About midway on the north side of the Plaisance was the Chinese Building here pictured. It was a structure typical of the Celestials, whose conceptions run largely to the grotesque. The interior, however, was infinitely more curious to the wondering eyes of visitors than the storied towers, gonfalons and gruesome imagery that characterized the exterior. The Chinese are remarkably superstitious and their gods are as precious to them as they were to Laban, and therefore those at the Fair had to have their Joss House, with its idols of horrid visage and elaborate decorations, squatted around in dim corners and on high platforms, like so many devils. In this same building also was a bazaar stocked with a thousand curiosities of Chinese manufacture, and a large theatre in which there were daily performances, by a troupe that was brought over from China to teach Americans some new features of dramatic art. The orchestra, too, probably expected to afford instruction to those not educated to an appreciation of Chinese harmonies—or noisy instrumentation.

CARAVANSARY IN THE GERMAN VILLAGE.—Among the mediæval curiosities within the grounds occupied by the German Village was an old Gasthaus, or Caravansary of the Fifteenth Century, that served the purpose of a restaurant for a while, and later was used as sleeping quarters for employes about the village. In the photograph herewith, the building is admirably pictured with members of the German Military Band on the veranda. It was a strange building, nor entirely reproductive of an ancient German Inn, for the wood carving was more modern, but the arrangement and general appearance was decidedly mediæval. The public was not generally admitted to the enclosure in which it stood, because the building was for private use after its unpopularity as a restaurant was discovered.

DOOR IN THE CATHEDRAL OF BORDEAUX.—The most elaborate architecture in church construction and adornment is to be seen in European Cathedrals, and particularly in those built during the Middle Ages. The marble sculpture work and the carvings in these are not excelled, or even approached, in modern Cathedrals. Reproductions, in plaster, of several of the more famous galleries, doors, tombs and effigies which adorn the interiors of the magnificent church edifices of Europe, were exhibited at the Columbian Exposition, of which the photograph herewith is an excellent example. The main feature in the picture is the door of the north transept in the Cathedral of Bordeaux, France. On the left is a reproduction of the Tomb of Frances II. and his consort, in the Cathedral of Nantes, and on the right is the Fountain of the Innocents in the same Cathedral. Both the mortuary statue and the fountain are attributed to Jean Cousin, but there is no certain proof who the sculptor was.

TWO FAMOUS PAINTINGS.—In the United States Section of the Fine Art Building were two paintings that drew the particular attention of visitors, and left an ineffaceable impression upon all who saw them. They are reproduced with good effect in the above photograph. The immense picture on the right, that covered nearly one entire side of the room in which it was exhibited, is by the brush of Carl Marr and entitled "The Flagellants." It represents a procession of these religious fanatics parading the streets of an Italian city in the Fourteenth Century, scourging their naked backs with bars of iron, encouraged to this self-inflicted punishment by the exhortations of priests. These barbaric scenes were common in nearly all European cities between the Thirteenth and the Sixteenth Centuries, until the Inquisition put a stop to them by burning several of the leaders at the stake. The large painting on the right is by Julian Story, and is entitled "M'lle De Sombreuil, an Episode of the French Revolution." The action of the picture is the heroic interposition of M'lle De Sombreuil to save the life of her husband from a Jacobin mob.

EXHIBIT OF PAINTINGS BY ARTISTS OF NORWAY.—The accompanying photograph is of a portion of the Norway Section in the Art Building, and the pictures shown are as follows: "A Mountain Pasture" (flock of sheep) is by Sinding, and the one directly above is Thoulow's "Retour de Travail," which conveys its own interpretation in the sorrowful attitude of the bereaved man. Next to the pasture scene is "Winter," by Skredsvig, and above it is "A Summer Day in Norway," by Groenvold. The portrait shown is of Sivert Nielsen, President of the Storthing (the Norwegian Congress). The large picture at the top of wall fronting the spectator represents a "Norwegian Fjord," and is by the brush of Hausteen, and next to it, towards the right, is one of Jorgensen's masterpieces, entitled "Out of Employment." There is a small picture near the centre of the hangings on the fronting wall representing "The Discovery of America by Lief Eriksson," from the brush of Krohg. The two pieces of marble statuary are, "A Sleeping Child," sculptured by Sinding; and "Hjördis," a patriotic Norwegian mother, by Tonnesen.

COLORADO'S STATE BUILDING.—The Centennial State was admirably and handsomely represented by a building 125 x 45 feet, whose principal features were two graceful towers that rose beside the main entrance to a height of eighty feet, terminating in belfries and pyramidal spires. Another feature of the Spanish moresque style, were hanging balconies and deep cornices, with a broad balcony over the triple arched entrance that were of decidedly Spanish suggestion. The interior was beautifully finished in natural woods, with fittings of marble and onyx, and there was a luxurious air of comfort in all its spacious rooms which invited visiting citizens from the State to repose, or to chatty conversation with friends. The cost of Colorado's Building was $35,000.

THE CALIFORNIA STATE BUILDING.—Next in size to Illinois' Capitoline structure was California's Building, which occupied a space 144 x 435 feet, and cost the sum of $75,000. It was an imposing as well as a curious building, of the Spanish Renaissance style, but somewhat imitative of the old missions erected by the Franciscan friars on the Pacific Coast in the seventeenth and eighteenth centuries. Everything about its exterior was suggestive of the antique, but withal in appearance it was very pleasing, and there was an irresistible charm about its roof garden, its solid towers, heavy arches, tiled roof, and low domes that were vivid reminders of the monasterial period, while every surrounding was rejuvenescent with the infusion of a progressive spirit. But as the character of the building was attractive, so were the exhibits which it contained both beautiful and interesting, for they included an almost infinite variety of fruits, cereals, and manufactured products that fully attested the greatness and advantages of the State.

THE COLUMBIAN BELL.—One of the curiosities exhibited at the Fair was a bell considerably larger than the famous Liberty Bell, which was for a while on exhibition before one of the entrances to Administration Building, where it rested when the above photograph was taken. It was an exhibit made by the Daughters of the Revolution, a patriotic organization of women, who for two years gathered souvenirs, trophies, and relics from every place in America, such as pieces of swords, buttons from military uniforms, bullets, muskets, copper coins and in short, every kind of metal thing that was a war remembrance, and then had the whole fused into one mass and cast, at Troy, New York, into the bell. It was originally the intention of the Daughters to have the bell make a circuit of the country and rung in every town, after which to send it abroad, but to their disappointment it awakened so little enthusiasm that the purpose was abandoned. So little was it talked about that comparatively few people at the Fair either saw or heard of it.

A PRIMITIVE TRAIN EXHIBITED BY THE NEW YORK CENTRAL RAILROAD.—A remarkable exhibit was made in the Transportation Building illustrating the evolution of the modern space-destroying locomotive and the palatial coaches that make travel a luxury. Among these numerous exhibits was the DeWitt Clinton train that ran on the New York Central Railroad in 1831, and which is here photographed. In those days stage coaches were the popular, because most comfortable, means of traveling, and which, it would appear, that railroad builders never hoped to supersede, unless by adapting them to tracks as well as to roadways. For which manifest reason the first cars were stage coaches with wheels adapted to rails. The locomotive was a monstrosity, as we view it now, using wood for fuel and barrels in which to carry the water supply. The highest rate of speed was fifteen miles an hour, but the average was ten or twelve when running. Frequent and prolonged stops to rest and repair the locomotive reduced the average speed to probably eight miles. Yet this was a remarkable improvement over the old stage coach and the canal boat. The DeWitt Clinton train is still in serviceable condition, but it would be better in a circus procession of curiosities than on the modern steel roadway.

A GROUP OF ALGERIANS.—The most picturesquely costumed people that were to be seen at the Fair were the Algerians, a group of the most prominent ones being shown in the photograph, with Ela Ganon, the Grand Patriarch, seated in the centre. There were many interesting features connected with the Algerian and Tunisian Village, chief of which was a theatre in which songs and dances peculiarly Algerian were executed, one of the dances, called the Assiiaeu, consisting of rhythmic contortions, which was intended to represent torture, which the name signified. Connected with the village were bazaars, in which bric-a-brac, tapestries and jewelry were sold, and in booths were Tunisian workmen manufacturing native clothing, daggers, swords, etc. The entire village was handsomely decorated with colored tiles brought from Algiers. There was also a Kabyle family in a separate tent, the members of which were constantly engaged spinning and weaving material for native fabrics, and in a Kiosk the natives manufactured candy that looked like wool and was nearly as palatable.

A GROUP OF SOUTH SEA ISLANDERS.—The picture herewith is of five natives of Wallis Island, a member of the Navigator Group, of which Samoa is the largest. As the illustration shows, they were a strong and athletic people, and would anywhere be regarded as specimens of perfect physical manhood. They lived while at the Fair in an enclosure with a company of Samoans, pictures of whom were given in portfolio No 1. Adjoining their village of open thatched huts was a theatre in which they gave three entertainments each day, and to which they attracted attention a half hour before each performance by beating on a hollow log and chanting a lugubrious and monotonous air. Their exhibition consisted of songs and dances, the former a chant and the latter a series of leaps and fugue movements. In their exercises the soles of their bare feet would strike the floor with a sound that resembled the stroke of a clapboard. and investigation showed that their feet were as hard as wood and perfectly insensible to prickings with a needle, or even to fire. The skin of their bodies was a clear yellow and so slick that it shone in the sunlight like polished leather. They were an amiable, vivacious, handsome and very agreeable people.

THE ALASKAN VILLAGE.—On the edge of South Pond, near the Shoe and Leather Building, and the Cliff Dweller's Exhibit, was a village of Alaska Indians, composed of some twenty persons. These people, representing the Arctic section of our domain, are peculiar in many ways; their social, domestic and religious customs being alike different from those of any other race or tribe. Prominent features of their villages are what are called by them Totem poles, high and grotesquely carved tree trunks which, though not regarded as divinities, are believed by the Alaskans to have the power to preserve the village against the machinations of evil spirits. They pay no homage to these images, nor even bestow upon them any care, so that if one tumbles down it is suffered to remain prostrate, because the Alaskans believe that each Totem pole is the embodiment of a ruling and beneficent spirit, and to interfere with it in any way would arouse its anger. These people subsist almost entirely by fishing, in which art they are wonderfully dextrous. Their large canoes are made from a single tree trunk, which is grouted chiefly by the use of fire. Their smaller crafts, called kyaks, are made of seal skin drawn tightly over a frame, and is never large enough for more than two persons.

THE LAPLAND COMPANY.—The entire company of Laplanders, including men, women, boys and babies, that were brought to the Columbian Exposition, are photographed in the above illustration. The manager of the company stands in the centre of the group, holding a Lapland cradle in his arm, and another baby is in the arms of its father, peeping out of its infantile housings of fur and reindeer skin. The costumes of the people are clearly shown, as are also their facial characteristics, their reindeer, and one of their curious, sharp-bowed and square-butted canoe sledges. In the foreground is a pet bear, which the Laps brought with them from their far-distant home, as a specimen of the wild animal life of their country. Lapland is now a Russian province, being a part of Northwest Russia, and, though being very far north, the climate is not so severe as that of the corresponding latitude in Siberia; but it is cold enough, the thermometer sometimes dropping as low as 50° below zero. The Laps are a brave people, but they are content to count their wealth in reindeer instead of in lands or money, the commercial instinct being little developed in them; nor are they generally ambitious, and though much more intelligent, they resemble, in some respects, the North American Indians, especially in their indifference to provision against future needs.

AN EXHIBIT OF FURNITURE FROM HINDOSTAN.—In a double pavilion, one part of which was constructed entirely of teak wood, and covering fifty feet front of one of the street aisles in Manufactures Building, was the very attractive display of India furniture, most exquisitely carved and beautifully inlaid with mother-of-pearl. It will be noticed by those who critically examine the photograph that the furniture is of the nature of a composite in style, combining, apparently, that of China, India and the English. This is due to the development and assimilation of tastes, the result of bringing together the commercial representatives of those three people, in which we observe that the English finally dominate. Among this model furnishing of the partially modernized East were charming and elaborately carved chairs, tables, lounges, book-cases, etc , some of teak, and others of sandal wood that perfumed with delicious odors the whole section. The curtains with which the walls were hung were likewise of India manufactures, and set off the furnished room to excellent advantage.

HANS CHRISTIAN ANDERSEN'S MEMORIAL SECTION.—A part of the Swedish display in Manufactures Hall was taken up by a reproduction of the library-room of Hans Christian Andersen, just as he left it when he entered the fairy land of his delightful imaginings and longings. Thousands of persons paid homage at that temporary shrine, thousands whose first impressions of the ideal were created by the beautiful fairy stories of that distinctively ideal man. One might almost imagine a glimpse of a sprite whisking out and in among the quaint chairs, tables, fireplace, or from behind the old pictures that gave a strange life to the walls. It was so real; there was the table upon which he wrote, the chair in which he sat, the lounge upon which he rested, the old floor clock that kept him company, and, indeed, all the accessories of his work, for everything had to him an individuality as well as a use. It was an ideal workshop and an ideal living-room for an idealist.

THE MAJOLICA VASE IN GERMANY'S EXHIBIT.—The gorgeous façade to Germany's section in Manufactures Building is described in another number of this serial. Our photograph here presents a view of the fine Daltons, Majolica wares, mural decorations, and a quarter of the façade, with one of its beautiful Saracen pillars. The principal feature here shown, however, is the magnificent Majolica Vase that stood upon the south newel and was the means of drawing thousands of people to the German exhibit. The vase stood twelve feet high, on an exquisitely carved pedestal, and was an object of extraordinary beauty, not alone for its lovely coloring, but also for the wonderful figures with which it was so lavishly and artistically decorated. A profusion of flowers and vines ran riotously up and down the vase, as if carelessly flung there by the mischievous cupids that were sporting about its sides, and luxuriating like butterflies in the bouquet that burst into richest bloom of wondrous coloring at the top. The value of this grandly magnificent vase was $10,000.

AN ARABIAN DROMEDARY RESTING.—In the streets of Cairo dromedaries were one of the sights, and were a delight to thousands who enjoyed the novelty and discomfort of a ride through the avenue on one of the strange beasts. In the Bedouin village there were three dromedaries, used for a different purpose, which were exhibited in all the richness of Oriental caparison. Sham battles, with Arab weaponry, lances, scimeters and long-barrelled guns, constituted the daily exhibitions, in which dromedaries took a spectacular part, sometimes ridden by red-turbaned merchants, and again by veiled women bespangled with trinkets pending from ears and clothes. The show was therefore illustrative of caravan and combat, and afforded both instruction and amusement, for the uniqueness of the exhibition was very attractive to the curious, while to those interested in the customs of strange people there was a practical lesson which was highly instructive and gratifying, in every movement of the actors as well as in the associated attractions which gave embellishment to the show.

PROCTOR'S MOOSE STATUES.—The photograph above was taken from a position near the northwest corner of Agricultural Building, looking across the South Lagoon towards Administration Building. The principal figures are two heroic Moose Statues, which stood on high pedestals, at the approach to a bridge over which passage was made between Agricultural Building and Machinery Hall. These splendid pieces of staff statuary were modeled by Proctor, who designed and executed many other conspicuous animal figures that adorned the grounds, and which were admired by every visitor that saw them. The figures, which were considerably larger than life size, were excellent simulations of the noble animal that is the monarch representative of wild forest life in the unreclaimed region of the great Northeast; a vanishing lord of the pineries and snow-lands of Maine. Duplicates of these also occupied pedestals at the approach to the bridge that spanned the lagoon between Horticultural Building and Wooded Island.

A SECTION OF THE GRAND COURT OF HONOR.—The view herewith is southward from the north Electric Fountain down the Lagoon towards the South Colonnade. On the right is seen a portion of Machinery Hall, and between is MacMonnies' Fountain, the Column of Victory, and Kemey's Deer. On the left is the west front of the great and beautiful Agricultural Building, and terminating the South Lagoon is the Obelisk and South Colonnade. The picture is bewildering in its beauty, conveying as it does a realistic impression of the grandeur of the Court of Honor and the glorious splendor which it revealed when all the fountains were set playing, throwing their streams in fantastic and shifting figures of mist, while the central basin poured its Niagara flood over circular terraces and rushed in tremendous swirls into the Lagoon.

BRIDGE OVER THE LAGOON, FACING THE GRAND BASIN.—The eye can never grow satiated feasting upon the transcendent glories and beauties that characterized the Court of Honor and the shores of the Grand Basin. Our view above is of the magnificent bridge over which visitors passed in going direct from Administration Building to Manufactures Hall, a distance of some three hundred yards. At either end of this splendid bridge were Galert's exquisite rostral columns of Neptune, so-called because the shafts were decorated with the bows, or beaks, of three ancient ships, while upon the summits were heroic statues of the noble sea-god. At the immediate bridge-approach were staff-figures of polar and grizzly bears, examples of the skillful and artistic modeling of Proctor and Kemys, beside the pedestals of which were flights of steps leading to the lagoon landing. The building across the Grand Basin is Agricultural Hall, which shows somewhat mistily because of its distance from the point of observation.

MINES AND MINING BUILDING.—Immediately northwest of Administration Building and extending its north front along the southwest lagoon, was the building devoted to the Mine and Mining exhibits. Its dimensions were almost exactly the same as those of Electricity Building, which stood beside it, viz.: 700 x 350 feet. The floor area of the structure was 8⅔ acres and the total cost was $265,000. The architect, Mr. S. S. Beman, very properly sacrificed imposing style to strength and adaptability, and the result was gratifying to a degree; yet in exterior appearance it harmonized well with the associated buildings as well as with the landscape of lagoon and island which it faced. The striking features of the architecture that caught the eye upon entering, was a gallery that encircled the interior, and a skylight extending the extreme length of the building, which flooded the whole nine acres of enclosed space with the clearest yet softest light. The objects that attracted largest attention in this building were: Montana silver statue that weighed 5000 pounds, the Castle of Chapultepec imitated in gold, a nugget of gold worth $41,000, a diamond mine, and a messenger from other worlds in the form of a meteorite that weighed 1015 pounds. The statue on the right is Proctor's Indian.

TURKS AND PERSIAN.—The photograph here given is of two European Turks and a Persian, the group being presented so as to show by comparison the difference in facial appearance and costumes between the two peoples. The Turks were merchants who conducted bazaars in the reproduced street of Constantinople, and the Persian, whose home is near the border of Syria, is likewise a member of the commercial guild of his own country. The three are represented in the attitude of negotiating a trade for some rich cloths, so as to better typify their occupations. People of the East are constitutionally tired or have corns on the soles of their feet, or at least it would appear that they had some weakness about the legs or feet, for they always seem to be sitting or reclining, and are apparently never in an upright position except when they are going somewhere and a palanquin is not convenient to hand.

A PERSIAN TAKING HIS COMFORTER.—From the far away country of Zoroastrianism, from the land of the lotus and the bulbul, which Moore has immortalized in his lay of the Fire Worshipers, come representatives, some with rich fabrics for commercial gain, and others to exhibit before World's Fair visitors the customs and costumes of the Persian people. Our picture above is that of a gentleman in afternoon costume indulging his after-dinner appetite with the solacing nargileh, which every defender of the faith in Persia is expected to use at least three times a day, and as much oftener as his means and inclination will allow. This pipe of the Orientals, for it is used by other Eastern peoples than the Persians, consists of a globe bottle that holds about a pint of water, capped by a long stem, on the top of which is the tobacco bowl. The smoke is drawn down into and through the water, and thence through a long flexible tube into the mouth of the smoker, as shown by the illustration.

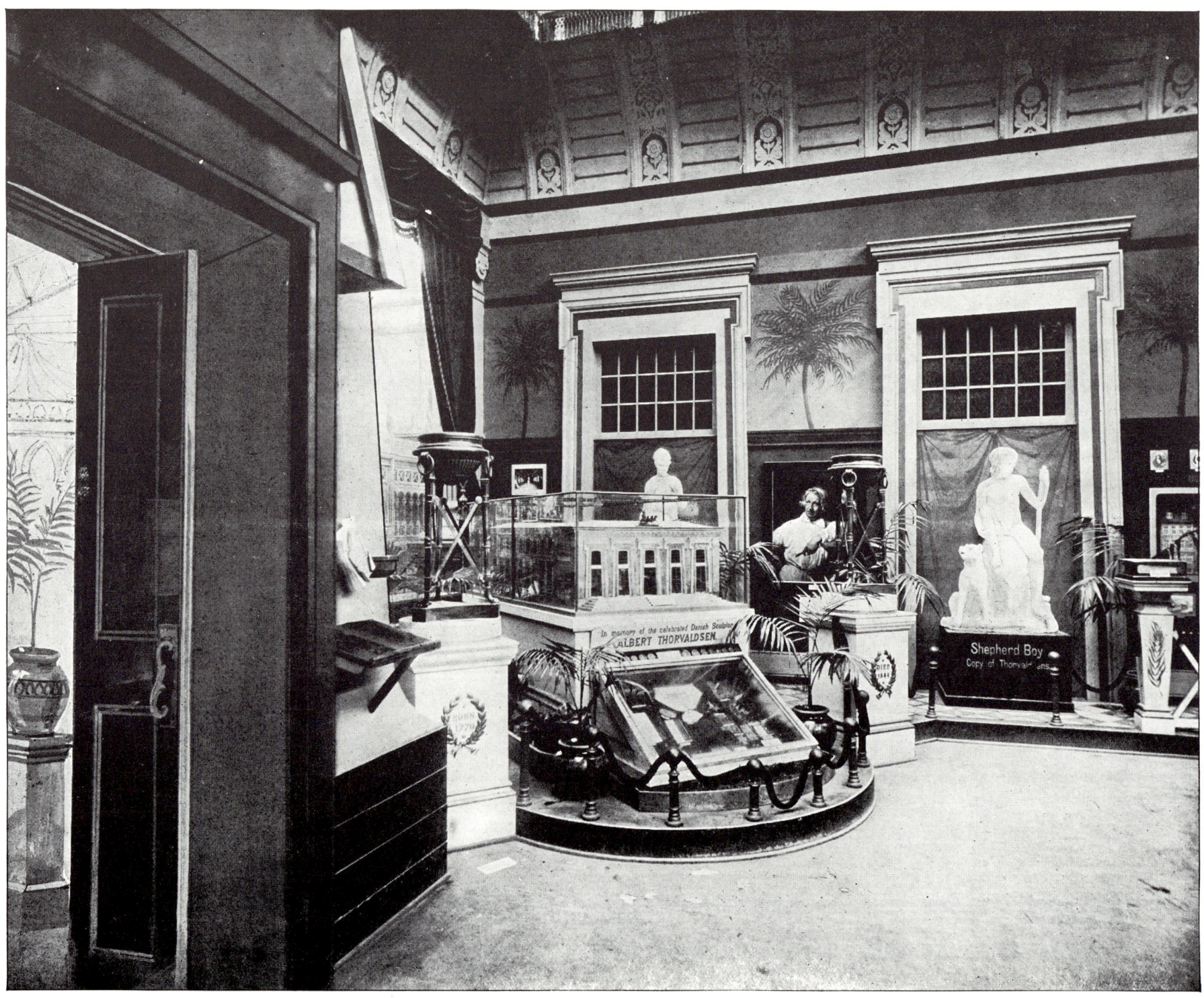

THORWALDSEN'S ART ROOM.—In the north façade of Manufactures Building was a pavilion divided into three parts, in one of which, and very near the room devoted to Hans Christian Andersen relics, was a small section of Denmark's display, in which plaster reproductions of famous Thorwaldsen sculptures were shown. His masterwork in marble, representing a shepherd boy, had the place of honor in the exhibit, but the memoria monuments that served to perpetuate him in the grateful remembrance of his countrymen were given such prominence, with other mortuary reminders, that the room had a rather funereal appearance, on which account, possibly, it was not largely visited. Adjoining the Thorwaldsen room was the Danish section, the walls of which were beautifully decorated with landscape paintings of parts of Denmark, Iceland, Greenland and the Danish West India colonies.

THE CLOCK TOWER AND FRENCH SECTION.—The picture above gives a very advantageous and distinct view of the great Central Clock Tower, and the imposing façade of the French government exhibit in Manufactures Building. The tower was 100 feet high, terminating with a globe cupola in which a dozen fine toned bells were hung, that rang out sweet chimes when the clock struck the hours, making music that resounded through the entire colossal hall. This clock gave the time not to Manufactures Building, but also to every department of the Fair, as it was run by electricity and connected by wire with all the large time-pieces within the grounds. On the right is seen the grand arched portal and wings of the magnificent French exhibit, which occupied 200 feet of front space along the central hall of the great building. Under the arch is rather indistinctly seen the heroic bronze statue of the French Republic, described in another number of this series, one of the most splendid pieces of statuary work ever brought to America, and one which World's Fair visitors will never cease to praise.

SOUTH FACADE OF THE ART PALACE.—Our picture shows to the best possible advantage the centre front of the Art Palace facing the North Lagoon, and the launch and gondola landings. The beautiful dome, 125 feet high, is slightly dwarfed by the perspective and by the removal of the figure of Victory which surmounted for a time the summit. The four figures standing immediately above the columns represent Architecture, Painting, Music and Sculpture, while winged females of grace and beauty flank the four representatives of art. A heroic statue of Minerva occupied a pedestal in front of the entrance, and to the left and right were gabled pediments supported by Caryatids, while alert lions guarded the approach. The sculpture pieces on façade and approach were by Martiny, Bauer and Proctor.

THE CANADIAN BUILDING.—Our northern neighbor was very well represented by an exceedingly pretty building, delightfully situated so as to command an expansive view of the lake. The total area covered was nearly 6000 feet, but the building proper was only fifty feet square, the rest of the space being covered by a porch ten feet wide that surrounded the house, with a corresponding veranda around the second story. The architecture of the building was of a subdued style, plain but inviting, while the swell front, that continued above the roof in the form of a balustraded tower, gave it a rather imposing, as well as a very handsome, appearance. The interior was beautifully finished in highly polished natural woods contributed by all the Dominion provinces. The structure cost $30,000, and was devoted to official purposes and as a meeting place for Canadian visitors.

BENEATH THE DOME OF HORTICULTURAL BUILDING.—In another number of this series is a picture and description of the immense Crystal Dome of Horticultural Building, under which were displayed the tall palms and bamboos that waved their feathery crests close to the ceiling of the lofty vault. There were hundreds of arboreal curiosities exhibited in this section of the building, many of which are native to foreign climes. Beautiful effects were also shown in terraced and suspended banks, green with mosses, ivies and creeping plants, while the charming realism of a forest illusion was greatly increased by the reproduction of a cave, before which ran a limpid brook that after winding its way across the section entered a grotto whose ceilings were hung with artificial stalactites that gleamed with fiery hues under dancing reflections of electric lights that made of it a hall of splendor.

COLUMBIAN STATUE IN THE ADMINISTRATION PORTAL.—One of the grandest pieces of statuary art that was seen at the Exposition occupied a conspicuous, as well as a commanding, position under the arch of the east portal of the Administration Building. And it is significant of woman's future, as it is of her ability to rise to the noblest conceptions, and to create forms of her brilliant fancies, that a woman should design and execute this chief monumental figure at the Fair. To Miss Mary T. Lawrence, of cosmopolitan fame, belongs the credit and honor of this splendid figure. Columbus is represented as just landing upon the shore of the New World, and planting the banner of Spain in the virgin soil, as a sign of Spanish acquisition. Over the arch are angels heralding the new faith, and on the pediment is an inscription announcing the date of sailing and discovery. On the sides of the portal are groups representing respectively, " Water Uncontrolled," and " Water Controlled." The sculptor of these groups was Karl Bitter.

THE SYRIAN LANCERS.—In an enclosure far up the Midway was an arena some five or six acres in extent in which Arabs and Syrians gave frequent exhibitions of furious riding, lance throwing and sword combats. The photograph presents two of the most expert lancers at the conclusion of their dangerous exercise, and was taken at that time in order to show how little was the fatigue the men and horses felt after undergoing the most violent exertion. The performance consisted of swift evolutions on horseback and the dexterous handling of lances that were twelve feet in length. The riders dashed at each other at a maddening pace, flourishing their ungainly weapons with fright-inspiring abandon, wheeling suddenly, countering thrusts, and while racing their animals to the utmost casting their lances at objects on the ground with unerring accuracy.

THE MICHIGAN LOGGING CAMP.—Close by the exhibit of pine logs made by the Michigan lumbermen, and near the south colonnade and saw-mill, was a typical Logging Camp, erected by the Nester Brothers of Baraga. This camp was a great curiosity to the thousands who visited and inspected it, because it seemed to be a genuine transplantation from dense pineries of the almost unexplored north section of Michigan. The building was twenty feet wide and seventy long, and was made entirely of pine logs, even to the roof and two jug-shaped chimneys. Here a company of lumbermen lived just as they do in the deep forests, except, perhaps, there was more order and less gaming. The men cooked, ate and slept in the building, using utensils identical with those which they employ when living in the dreary isolation of their forest quarters. The photograph above gives a perfect likeness of the building at the Fair, and of its immediate neighborhood.

A TURKISH AND A PERSIAN SWORDSMAN.—Nearly all the Orientals are skillful fencers and duellists with the sword, and their accomplishments with this weapon have been famous since Richard Cœur de Lion attempted to wrest Jerusalem from Saladin. In no city in the world were such splendid blades manufactured as in Damascus, and the Syrian secret of tempering steel was ever so jealously guarded that it is now one of the lost arts. These fencers of the East, among whom the Turks cannot be properly included, prefer shields of hippopotamus hide to those of metal, since the former are equally impervious to the sword and much lighter; neither do they use a large shield, but usually one of about eighteen inches diameter, and it is truly astonishing how dexterously they interpose it to every thrust or stroke. In the exhibitions given at the World's Fair these combatants fought with a spirit that admirably simulated earnestness, attacking with fierceness and delivering their strokes with a rapidity and vigor that appeared to threaten serious injury to one of the fighters, yet no accident happened in any of the conflicts.

HINDOSTANEE DELEGATES TO THE CONGRESS OF RELIGIONS.—It was a splendid idea, having its conception in a desire to know the truth, and in a spirit of liberal concession and deference to the beliefs of others, that led to the assembling at Chicago, of a convocation of representatives of all modern religions. Such a thing had been suggested before, in the Fall of Pompeii, but it was idealistic, like Moore's Utopia; practically, such an idea never before bore fruit, and the fairness and kindly feeling that animated the congress is prophetic of the time when the brotherhood of man will be universal. The delegates from India, representing the Hindostan race and the Brahmanistic religion, attracted larger interest, and commanded closer attention from the attendants than any other representatives. These gentlemen from the land of Buddha and of magnificent temples, were polished and learned, and a majority of them spoke English with a charming accent and accuracy. They not only explained in a most fascinating manner the tenets of their doctrines, but addressed the convention on the literature of the East and its relation to the books of the Bible, tracing the broad humanity, the reverent feeling, the common fatherhood that is the actuating essence of all religions. Pictures of five of the most eminent Hindostanee delegates are given above.

THEIR HONEYMOON.—In another photograph this same happy Javanese couple are represented, but in a more prosaic attitude. Here they are shown in the beatitude of their honeymoon. The young bride wears an expression of the highest felicity, a feeling which her husband undoubtedly shares, but as he is having his picture taken he considers it more manly to assume an air of indifference, as though getting married were an every-day occurrence with him. Bridegrooms among our own people very often try to disguise their happiness in the same way, and succeed quite as poorly. The little wife, on the contrary, is bubbling over with joy, and doesn't care who knows it, she is trying her best to take care of the first precious husband she ever had, as she can never love another man in the whole world. Thus do we see the close kinship in feeling of all mankind. The husband wears a coat, shirt and cuffs, which are not a part of his usual costume, and these he will discard when he returns to his island home.

A VIEW OF THE FINISHED FRONT OF HORTICULTURAL BUILDING.—In another number of this series is an illustration of the Horticultural Façade taken before the building was entirely completed and before the basin of water-plants in front was finished. The view above shows the central entrance and crystal dome of the great building, with World's Fair visitors pouring into the gigantic conservatory where was exhibited nearly every specimen of the plant life of the world. The sculpture of the façade is very beautiful and worthy of critical examination. Running around the entire building is a frieze representing cupids at play, on the pediments of the arch are two figures, one of a farmer, and the other of a milkmaid. The principal sculptural figures, however, are two groups on the columns of the façade, the one on the right portraying a Battle of Flowers, and that on the left allegoric of the Sleep of the Flowers. All the sculpture work was by Lorado Taft.

THE ILLINOIS BUILDING.—As the State of Illinois had the very distinguished honor of having the great Columbian Exposition held within her borders, and to the aid of which she made an appropriation of $1,000,000, larger than the contribution of any other State, to her was conceded the right of selecting the choicest site upon which to erect her representative building. She chose a central position, around which all the other State buildings were located, and upon that spot she erected a mammoth and magnificent structure, costing $250,000. The dimensions of the building were 160 x 450, and the style was Capitoline, being, in fact, a reproduction of the State House at Springfield, exact to the minutest exterior details. The interior was, of course, adapted to the several displays made of the manufactures and agricultural productions of the State, which were very large, and in every respect as creditable to her wealth and importance as was the splendid building in which they were exhibited.

THE HAYTIAN BUILDING.—The first building completed and dedicated at the World's Fair was that erected by the Republic of Hayti, which was ready for the reception of guests as early as January 2, 1893. The dedicatory address was delivered by Fred Douglass, ex-minister to Hayti, at the request of President Hypolite, who has ruled the turbulent population of that island with marked results for good. Hayti was discovered by Columbus during his first voyage and named Hispaniola, or New Spain, because of the hospitable welcome he received from its inhabitants and the marvelous beauty and fertility of the country. It was from a port of this delightful, paradisaic island, however, that he was afterward sent back to Spain in chains, the luxuriance and wealth of the land arousing contention among the jealous, avaricious and malevolent voyagers that led to a conspiracy to compass his destruction. Hayti reveres the memory of Columbus and so zealously guards his fame that the government still claims his remains, despite the dispute that they were long ago removed to Havana. The cost of the Haytian Pavilion was $20,000.

THE COWBOY.—A heroic piece of staff statuary representing a "Cowboy" was set upon the border of the west lagoon between the Transportation Building and Choral Hall, and immediately facing it was a companion piece of equal size of an Indian, with hand shading the eyes as he sweeps the prairie for friend or foe. The attitude of the Cowboy is that of a fierce rider across the plains, who at a sudden discovery of danger ahead draws up his horse with a turn that sets him back almost upon his haunches. There is great spirit and strength in the figures, but as the work was to endure for only a six months the sculptor did not finish the details of his model, or left the execution to assistants who failed thoroughly to complete the work. Nevertheless, the figures satisfied the less critical and even excited the admiration of a large number. The sculptor of these two immense pieces was Proctor, whose creations included a number of other heroic figures distributed about the grounds.

JOSEPH AND HIS BOOM-DE-AY DONKEY.—Those who visited the streets of Cairo, in the Plaisance, will quickly recognize the picture above. Among the many attractions and features of the Cairo thoroughfare were camel leaders and donkey drivers, in admirable imitation of Egyptian street scenes. An important difference between a camel and a donkey, resulting no doubt from a perverted instinct, through the difference of association, is that one may be led while the other must be driven. Our photograph herewith represents an Egyptian boy named Joseph, sitting astride of his demure little beast, known to Plaisance visitors as Boom-de-ay. Joseph was as much of a character as his woefully lazy donkey, the two affording infinite amusement from morning until night by a display of their singularly comical traits. Poor little Boom-de-ay was always under Joseph's lash, for though he made no objection to being mounted, nothing would move him but the Egyptian boy's ejaculations and a skillfully applied cudgel. During the Fair more than 3000 people of both sexes and nearly all ages rode this donkey through the Cairo street.

A GROUP OF ARAB HORSEMEN.—Arabia is a wild country, swept by hot winds and burning sands, but the disadvantages of soil and climate have promoted hardihood and courage in the natives who seem to thrive upon harsh conditions. They are the Ishmaelites and Amalekites of the Old Testament, the rough riders, and often the scourge of the desert, whose feats of horsemanship have for ages been wonders of human daring and possibilities. A large company of Arabs was brought to the Fair and assigned to a spacious arena in which to exhibit their amazing feats of riding, leaping, lance-throwing and sword-fencing. A part of the company is shown in the above picture, taken on their practice grounds, in full accoutrement and horse-trappings just before giving an exhibition. Nothing appeared to be more perilous than their savage riding, and the furious display which they made while wheeling and cavorting in the quickest and strangest way, bringing their swift animals up with a turn so sharp as to drive them to their haunches, and then turning short while at a furious pace so that the horses often appeared to be thrown upon their sides. All this while the Arabs were shooting their guns, flourishing their scimiters, and darting their lances with what appeared to be the greatest abandon and shocking recklessness, yet for all this accidents were very few and of little consequence.

A VILLAGE OF PENOBSCOT INDIANS.—The ethnological congress, composed of representatives of many tribes, from nearly every quarter and nation, could not be confined to the Midway Plaisance for lack of space, so a number of villages of uncivilized peoples were given places within the Fair Grounds proper. Among these latter were four families of Penobscot Indians, whose village quarters occupied an area of some 5000 feet on the borders of the south pond, close by the intramural railway. These people are a relic of the famous Five Nations who once were masters of the whole northeast, and played such an important part in the French and Indian war of 1754. The Penobscots, that now number about 300 souls, live upon a small reservation near Old Town, in Maine. They have never departed from their old custom of living in birch-bark tents, notwithstanding the severity of the climate to which they are exposed, and the examples of comfortable dwellings by which they are surrounded. They hunt and fish in season, but scarcity of game has caused them to adopt other means of subsistence. They are exceedingly skillful in the production of fine basket work, moccasins, snowshoes, bows and arrows, and birch-bark canoes, by the sale of which they are able to supply their small needs.

A SOUTH SEA ISLAND BUNGALOW.—The South Sea Islanders at the Exposition were from Upolu, the second largest island of the Navigator Group, which is noted for its lofty mountains and fertile valleys. Apia is its capital, and is a city of no small importance, situated at the head of an oval bay on the north coast. Near it is the island of Tutuila, which is almost cut in two by the harbor of Pango-pango, in which several men-of-war and more than 200 sailors were lost in the great storm which swept that coast in 1889. Many of the islanders have been Christianized through missionary effort, but the old superstitions still prevail largely among the interior people, who are believers in totemism, a form of transmigration and incarnate spirit worship. Owls are their principal totem, in which they believe resides a ruling spirit, that is usually the soul of some traditional chief. The bungalow, or hut, shown above, was built by the Samoan villagers at the Fair, and was a reproduction of a native council house, or village hall. It was thatched with banana leaves, and "weather-boarded" with sections of plaited cocoanut fibre.

MICHIGAN LUMBERMEN'S REMARKABLE EXHIBIT.—Near the South Colonnade and Amphitheatre, was a novel exhibit which excited no little wonderment. It was a truck upon which was piled fifty immense white pine logs cut from the North Michigan pineries. These logs constituted a single load that was hauled on one sled by the Nester Brothers of Baraga from the forest where the trees were cut, to Ontonagon River. They were then rafted to a point on the Duluth, South Shore and Atlantic Railroad, where they were shipped on nine freight cars to Chicago, where they were loaded onto a truck, to illustrate the manner in which they were first taken from the pinery. The weight of the load, which was drawn by a single span of horses, was 145 tons, and the number of square feet was 36,055. Adjacent to this immense tower of logs was a Logger's Camp, which was a part of the Lumbermen's exhibit, a log cabin 20 x 70 feet, in which a number of loggers lived as they do in the pinery. Near by was also a big sawmill, where all the latest machinery was in operation converting pine logs into lumber, much of which entered into the construction of the World's Fair buildings.

TWO REPRESENTATIVES OF THE SIOUX NATIONS.—The space allotted for the villages of the Indian nations was on the north side of the west end of Midway Plaisance, a very large enclosure protected against the view from the outside by a high board fence. Within this space was a grand encampment and confraternity of blanket Indians, where the tents of Sioux, Pawnees, Blackfeet and Cheyennes were separated by nothing but cloth and tent-pins, an association never seen upon the plains, where deadly hatred is characteristic of the tribes, and an exchange of flying arrows is the only intercourse. The largest representation was from the Sioux nation, the most powerful of Indian tribes, whose valor and numbers wrought Custer's annihilation in 1876. Our illustration is one of two Sioux men, whose style of dress shows the result of contact with civilization. In earlier years their raiment was principally a breech-clout and blanket, but progress has effected changes, which, though gradual, will in a few years more eliminate every appearance of savagery in the dress and customs of the plains Indians. They still wear the hair long and braided, and many decorate their persons with eagle feathers and quills; but hat, coat, pants, and even shoes are not so very rare among the Sioux, even when on their reservation, and with schools and experimental farms they are approaching citizenship, though slowly.

THESA, A SINHALESE WOMAN.—Nearly every country of the world had its representatives at the Fair, and a Congress of Nations was therefore one of its chief attractions. Many specimens of the semi-civilized and barbaric races were quartered in villages erected by themselves along the Midway Plaisance, while others were similarly housed within the Fair Grounds proper, so that the visitor was almost constantly meeting with dusky strangers whose queer raiment indicated their foreign nativity. The World's Congress of Religions brought to the Fair several distinguished representatives of the Orient, among whom those from India were probably the most learned and interesting. Ceylon was not omitted from this number, for she sent a representative in the person of a charming lady named Thesa, whose picture is here given, taken while she was reclining upon a rich rug, as is the custom of the Sinhalese people when resting or taking their meals. She belonged to the high social caste, and was also a disciple of Buddha, whose teachings she came to the Fair to explain and expound. She was highly educated and had traveled extensively with her husband, both of whom spoke English quite fluently.

A SOUTHWEST VIEW OF MANUFACTURES BUILDING.—The largest building that was ever reared by architectural genius was that constructed in which to house the displays of Manufactures and Liberal Arts. The Coliseum in Rome had a seating capacity of 100,000, but that was an amphitheatre without roof and therefore presented no architectural difficulties. Manufactures Hall was a complete building, occupying thirty-one acres of ground, covering a rectangular space 1687 x 787 feet, and the grand arches, therefore, had an uninterrupted stretch of more than 250 yards. In its construction there was used 17,000,000 feet of lumber, 12,000,000 pounds of steel, 2,000,000 pounds of iron, 589,170 feet of glass, and the cost was $1,727,431. Under the Central Hall, which was without a single pillar to support its roof, 75,000 people could be seated, and even then each person would have six square feet of space, while the entire floor space was sufficient to comfortably accommodate at one time 300,000 persons. The architect of this greatest of modern world's wonders was George B. Post, of New York. The height of the building was 212 feet 9 inches. The style was plain and necessarily modern, because there was nothing that it could have been patterned after.

WATERFALL OF THE COLUMBIAN FOUNTAIN.—The photograph herewith pictures the wonderful MacMonnies' Fountain while throwing its Niagara of water over the terraces and pouring its limpid flood into the Grand Basin. A more magnificent sight has been rarely witnessed, which was particularly gorgeous when the leaping waters were lighted up at night by a thousand multi-colored electric lights. The cost of operating the Fountain was one hundred dollars per hour, so great was the volume of water it discharged. The building shown in the illustration is Agricultural Hall, which, next to Manufactures and Liberal Arts Building, was the largest and most expensive structure on the grounds. The Fountain was second in size to the famous one at Versailles, the largest in the world.

THE VICTORIA HOUSE.—Simplicity of taste was exhibited in the design of Great Britain's World's Fair Building, but it was not lacking in elegance, nor in that quiet beauty which is a manifestation of comfort and true grace. The structure, unlike nearly all the other buildings, was a substantial one, the first story being of red brick and heavy terra cotta trimmings, and the second of interlaced timbers of a style that was common in the time of Henry VIII. The building had a preferred location, as it was very near the lake beach, and afforded an excellent view of nearly all the Fair Grounds as well as of the lake. The interior was elegantly finished and luxuriously furnished, as the building was reserved for the Commissioners of Her Majesty's Government, and visitors were not encouraged to make it a meeting place. The dimensions of Victoria House were 60 x 100, and the cost was $80,000.

THE FRENCH BUILDING.—The building which France erected in honor of the Fair was located on the lake front near the Victoria House, and was pretentious to a degree as compared with England's Building. In dimensions it was 250 x 175 feet, and consisted of two pavilions connected by a semi-circular colonnade, which enclosed a beautiful lawn with a splendid bronze fountain in the centre, facing the lake. In the north pavilion were exhibited a large number of gifts that had been made to Lafayette, together with many relics and mementoes of that great Frenchman who fought with Washington for American independence. In the south pavilion were displayed objects that interested the largest number of visitors, as it was a veritable rogues' gallery, wherein were shown portraits of famous criminals, and the methods employed to identify them by Paris police authorities. A large relief group, emblematic of the three French graces, Liberty, Equality and Fraternity, adorned the ends of the pavilions, with a couchant lion and palm branch beneath the groups, significant of the desire for peace but the power to defend. The cost of the French structure was $100,000.

ANOTHER VIEW OF THE FRENCH SCULPTURE EXHIBIT.—Some of the figures that are shown in the above photograph are to be seen in another picture already described, as the scene herewith is an extension of the French Sculpture Section in Art Hall. The chief marble figure, on the right, is that of Falguiere's allegoric statue of the French Republic. On the extreme left is an exquisite marble by Michael representing Aurora lifting the veil of night from her sight. Nearby is another piece by the same sculptor entitled "The Blind Man and the Paralytic." The nude figure lying down is a charming statue by Gaudez, entitled, "The Nymph Echo." Most of the other pieces are shown and mentioned elsewhere in this series.

A HOUSE IN THE JAVANESE VILLAGE.—Almost in the centre of the Javanese Village stood the dwelling shown in the illustration, a typical East India home, where little shelter is required except against rain. These buildings were all made of bamboo pillars and rafters, with interweavings between, for the walls, of split bamboo and palm leaves. They were very light and airy, but strong enough to resist a hurricane. Some beautiful designs were made by plaiting different colored bamboo splits, the black and brown strips being produced by scorching. All the fencing that enclosed the village was also made of bamboo, the pieces being joined by thongs of the same material in a most ingenious way. Unlike many other islanders, the people of Java are scrupulously clean in their habits and always polite, ready to satisfy the curiosity of strangers, and equally deferential and kindly to one another. Their wants are few and these are abundantly supplied by the products of their exceedingly fertile fruit-bearing island.

STATUARY AND CHURCH ARCHITECTURE EXHIBITED BY FRANCE.—France has maintained her supremacy in the Art world for many centuries, and the exhibition made by her great artists at the World's Fair indicates that she will continue to hold the artist's mace of sovereignty for a long while to come. In her collection at the Exposition she did not confine her display to statues and paintings, but presented examples of the marvelous church sculpturing for which she is renowned, and thus covered the entire field of art. In the photograph above are to be distinguished a reproduction of the door and west façade of the Cathedral of Aix, built in the sixteenth century, one of the most wonderful specimens of church sculpturing in the world. There are also shown the effigy of "Philippe VI., King of France," a statue of "Pope Leo XIII.," a marble group of the "Three Graces," "Diana," and a statue of "M. Patenotre," French Ambassador to the United States.

ANOTHER VIEW OF THE ITALIAN SECTION IN ART HALL.—Some of the figures to be seen in the above photograph are shown in a companion photograph picturing another view of the same section. The large marble figure in the foreground is a plaster representing "Icarus," by Paoli, and other statues noticeable are, "Satyr Unmasked," by Nelli, and "Stolen Pleasures," by Garibaldi. The pictures seen in this part of the exhibit are chiefly portraits of living persons, by artists who are still seeking reputations. This portion of the section is not so attractive as other parts illustrated in this series, but no room in the Art Hall was destitute of attractions, for never before in the history of the world was there gathered for exhibition such a magnificent and extensive collection of paintings and statuary.

NORTH SIDE OF THE GRAND BASIN.—Those who have an eye for the beautiful, and those who can appreciate the splendid works of genius, can never tire looking at and contemplating the magnificent productions of the artists who made the World's Fair a magic city of astounding splendor. It represented the joint result of lavish munificence and pre-eminent talent in all the constructive arts. Imagination never pictured a more extravagant scene of poetic grandeur than that presented in sublime reality by the marvelous beautification of the shores of the Grand Basin, which by a transformation as marvelous as that wrought by magician made the marsh of Jackson Park blossom with the most bewildering glories of artistic conceptions. The picture here presented is taken from the corner of Electricity Building and shows the bridge which spanned the lagoon at the south end of Manufactures Hall. In the centre stands the monolithic column that represented Navigation, and beyond are the graceful contours of the Peristyle, Temple of Vesta, Casino, and statue of the Republic, while at the end of the bridge is seen the arch leading to the south loggia of Manufactures Building, and the easy flight of steps which conducted to one of the boat landings on the lagoon.

BRIDGE OVER THE SOUTH LAGOON.—The photograph here presented affords an excellent view of the bridge that connected Machinery Hall and the Agricultural Building, and also a back-ground vision of the Grand Basin, southeast corner of Manufactures Building, Music Hall, Statue of the Republic, Temple of Vesta and the Peristyle. Prominent features in the picture are the South Lagoon corner front of Agricultural Building, and one of the rostral columns that has been elsewhere described. The statues of Buffaloes and Moose, to be seen at the termini of the bridge, were modeled by Kemeys. The picture is a beautiful one, exhibiting, as it does, an expanse of the most artistic section of the Fair Grounds. The lagoon seen most prominently in the photograph ran south to the Egyptian Obelisk and north to the Art Building, the entire way being alive with electric launches, gondolas and other pleasure crafts during the Exposition.

SCENE IN THE AUSTRIAN SECTION OF PAINTINGS.—Austria was fully represented in the art collection by the best paintings produced by her most eminent artists. There was also great artistic taste displayed in the decoration of the section, and in the arrangement of the pictures, upon which the light was made to fall in the softest and most effective manner. The photograph herewith represents only a small part of the display, yet it shows two of the finest paintings that were to be seen at the Fair. Chief of these is Huber's superb equestrian picture of Washington, admirably shown in the photograph. The other is Makart's allegoric representation of The Five Senses, to be seen on the right. The other pictures are too indistinct to justify particular mention.

A CORNER OF THE GERMAN CASTLE.—In Southern Germany there is still to be seen an occasional relic of old feudal times, in ivy-covered walls of ancient castles that gave shelter and security to masters of appanages acquired by conquest rather than through gift of the crown. The German Government happily decided to reproduce, for the benefit and instruction of World's Fair visitors, a Castle of the Middle Centuries, and to this end was assigned some acres of ground on the Midway Plaisance upon which to erect a mediæval building. Faithfully the designs of the government were carried out, with the result of producing a structure that aroused very great curiosity, as well as the liveliest interest, especially among those who have read of baronial halls, moat-surrounded castles, and the vassal armies of feudal lords. Within the building were museums of antique weaponry and ancient costumes, carrying us back to the time of the Franks and Huns, the proud and bearded conquerors of Rome.

THE LION FOUNTAIN AND OBELISK.—One of the prettiest views within the Exposition Grounds was that which is preserved in the perfect picture here presented. The space covered is not large, but within it is gathered many of the most splendid architectural and sculptural productions of the Exposition. In the foreground, which shows the lagoon fronting Machinery Building, are two of Paul Hull's statues of harnessed horses and coatless workmen, representing Industry. Across the lagoon is the west end of Agricultural Building, prominent on the top of which is a group typifying the four races. At the south end of the basin is the Columbian monument and fountain. On the four corners of the plinth are eagles, the bird of American sovereignty, and on the base are as many lions, sculptured by Waagen, significant of strength. South of the monolith is the colonnade, whose wide centre arch gave access to a large amphitheatre used for a while for cavalry manœuvres, and later was the arena in which the horse-show was held. The jaguars guarding this arched entrance were by Kemeys and Proctor.

A LAPLAND FAMILY.—The above photograph represents the family of King Bull, who was the most prominent character in the Lapland village. His wife is in the centre holding her infant in a reindeer-skin cradle, from beneath the hood of which its merry little eyes twinkle forth. On the right is his brother-in-law, and before the older members are three children, two boys and a girl, that complete the family. It will be noticed with some curiosity that every one of the party is very much squint-eyed, a habit which, it may be explained, the Laps acquire because of the glare that is reflected by the vast fields of snow over which they travel and by which they are surrounded during six months in the year. Nature has also assisted them to withstand, in a measure, this strain upon their sight by giving them small eyes and deep arches, but this provision does not entirely prevent diseases arising from the sun's glare upon the snow, for a large proportion of the Lap population are afflicted with imperfect sight and diseases of the eye.

RUINS OF YUCATAN.—For the archæologist nothing else exhibited at the Exposition had such a fascinating interest as the Ruins of Yucatan. These were located near the Dairy Building in the southeast part of the grounds, and occupied a space fifty feet square. To those who looked upon these habitation relics of an extinct race, they appeared to be composed of a rough concrete, but in truth the ruins were exact reproductions made of staff from papier-maché moulds, taken from the original ruins of Uxmal, under the direction of E. H. Thompson, U. S. Consul at Yucatan. They were therefore exact reproductions in appearance and size, even to the minor detail of living cactus growing in the interstices of the walls and about the base. Who were the people that built the splendid palaces of which these are the ruins? They were ruins centuries old when Columbus first landed on San Salvador, and were probably courts of royal magnificence when our Saviour was teaching in the synagogues, and traveling foot-weary through the rocky valleys of Judea. If we could but know the past we might better be able to prophesy as to the future.

GYMNASIUM IN THE CHILDREN'S BUILDING.—A unique feature of the World's Fair was the representation accorded to women and the munificent arrangement that was made for the care of children. These had been a secondary consideration at previous international fairs, here they were first. The Children's Building was a pretty and ample structure located between the Woman's and Horticultural Buildings, under the fostering care, as it were, of the mothers who gave their energies to and contributed of their means to make the Fair an unexampled success. In the Children's Building there were many departments for physical as well as mental training, but in none other was there so much enthusiasm as in the gymnasium beautifully pictured above. Here was provided every kind of machine and mechanical means for developing the physique and muscles of both girls and boys, and their performances were a tireless exhibition that furnished amusement to thousands of visitors as well as to themselves.

THE **SPANISH GOVERNMENT BUILDING.**—On the Lake-front, between the buildings of Germany and Canada, was the Spanish Government Building, with a frontage of eighty-five, and a depth of ninety-five feet. It was a three-fourths reproduction of the Silk Exchange at Valencia, which was built in the year that Columbus set sail on his first voyage (1492). The section shown in the photograph is the hall and tower, which a century ago was used as a prison for the confinement of defaulters. Eight large columns support the roof of the hall, and a circular stairway afforded means for reaching the top of the tower, that rose to a height of sixty-five feet. The building was used by the Spanish Commission in which to receive visitors, and was likewise a Columbian museum, where were shown many valuable relics, such as some of Columbus' letters, a sword that belonged to Isabella, also one which Cortez carried during his invasion of Mexico, some pieces of ancient Spanish cannon, etc.

A PORTION OF THE FRONT OF MACHINERY HALL.—A little more than one-half of the east front of the Palace of Mechanic Arts (Machinery Hall) is shown in the illustration. The style of architecture is Spanish Renaissance, which is emphasized by the spires, in the cupola of two of which bells were hung whose wild music broke over all the tumult of the swarming grounds. The view presents a section of the colonnade at the south end of the basin, and also the Egyptian Obelisk, which was a reproduction of the one in Central Park, New York. The picture is not beautiful with charming buildings and lovely waterway, but is diversified with magnificent examples of the sculptor's classic art. On the balustrade of Machinery Hall we see five of the ten figures representing the sciences, and in the pediment is indistinctly observed a group of inventors, while upon the spire is a winged figure of Victory, of all which Waagen was the sculptor. The harnessed horses on the approach were by Proctor, as were also the bulls on the left, but the stately elk on the pedestal was by Kemys.

ROTUNDA OF THE GOVERNMENT BUILDING.—The most artistic and pleasing portion of the Government Building was the elegant and spacious rotunda rising clear to the dome, a height of 150 feet. The decoration was by mural paintings of famous incidents in American history and scenes in our largest cities, thus making it representative of the whole country. In the centre of the rotunda was a hollow section of one of the largest trees that grew in the Maraposa grove of red woods, California. The interior was brilliantly lighted by means of incandescent lights, and a platform at the top of the trunk was reached by a winding stairway inside. The chamber walls were covered with photographs, chiefly of the grove from which the tree trunk was cut, and illustrations of how it was conveyed to the Fair and set up. In the rotunda were eight alcoves, wherein were displayed a great quantity of interesting colonial relics, among which was the first Bible brought to this country, in 1620, the pipe which Miles Standish smoked, the fife of Benedict Arnold, Burgoyne's spur, a piece of the torch which Putnam used when he entered the wolf's cave, and many others of scarcely less interest.

THE EXHIBIT OF WINDMILLS.—Those who made a trip on the Intramural Railway to the southeast terminus could not fail having their attention drawn to the wonderful display of every imaginable make of windmill that covered some five acres of space with whirling wings and humming voices. These machines not only caught the wind in their arms in sensuous sportiveness, but they served a hundred useful purposes to which steam is most generally applied. In the workshops for which these windmills furnished the power there were lathe-turning, planing, corn-shelling, feed-cutting, grain-separating, threshing, wood-sawing, generating electricity, and scores of other things, demonstrating the wide scope of usefulness of the windmill aside from water-pumping and grinding which for years was the limit of its application.

A REPRESENTATIVE OF THE SOUDAN.—The photograph herewith is that of a Soudanese merchant from Khartoum, where the chivalrous and heroic Gordon met his death. This man, though a full-blood Ethiopian, had seen something of the outskirts of semi-civilized Upper Egypt and been in contact with officials of the Khedive, whose costumes he thought so well of as to partly adopt. Thus he appears in clothes of the high-caste Egyptians. He possessed great intelligence, as his features indicate, and was a wealthy man in his country, being a large dealer in corn, goats, and cattle, and was formerly a slave merchant, but this latter business was partially destroyed by restrictive measures enforced by the young Khedive, so that it is no longer profitable.

A PORTION OF THE ITALIAN STATUARY EXHIBIT.—The view here shown is a small section of Italy's splendid display of statuary work, among which were to be found many figures that Angelo himself, were he now living, might stop his chiseling to admire. At the left side of the picture is Apolloni's jocund and exquisite statue of "America," represented as a "telephone girl," if we are permitted to so designate a classical creation. The figure adjoining is "The Poor Flower Girl," by Bardi; and the statue next to that is "The Kiss," by Bottinelli. On the right is a marble bust of Julia Ward Howe, and a fine character statue entitled "A Martyr," by Apolloni and Argenti respectively. On the walls are the following paintings: Heads of a bull and a tiger, by Lanetti; "Flirtation," by Wolf; "Vanity," by Rinaldi, and "Love and Curiosity," by Guerrieri.

THE COLD STORAGE FIRE.—The World's Fair will for ages be regarded as the greatest and most significant event in the peace history of America, but the jubilation of that immensely important and magnificent national enterprise is clouded by one of the most shocking calamities that has ever befallen any section of our country, and the close marked by an assassination of Chicago's mayor that shrouded the spirit of gratulation with the deep pall of mourning. These two tragic happenings will be indelible remembrances of the Columbian Exposition, as they are a part of its history. Our photograph above pictures the dreadful holocaust that occurred at two o'clock on the afternoon of July 10, 1893, when the Cold Storage Building, that stood at the southwest corner of the Fair grounds, a structure of highly inflammable material, with high towers at the corners, and a higher one in the centre, took fire and in a remarkably short while was wrapped in the arms of the red demon. The alarm was promptly responded to by the fire company, and as the flames were discovered to be confined at first to the centre tower, the brave firemen, with all possible haste, ascended with hose to its summit. Before the danger of their position became known the rapidly eating flames burst out below them and cut off retreat, save by the perilous expedient of jumping. Sixteen brave fellows found a funeral pyre where duty had thus called them.

EXHIBIT OF THE RELICS OF THE CLIFF DWELLERS.—In the southeastern part of the Fair Grounds, near the Yucatan Ruins, was a reproduction of Battle Rock Mountain, Colorado, represented in the photograph. The interior was reached through a cavernous portal on the north side, and the visitor was introduced to a large exhibit of the mummified remains and domestic relics of the Cliff-Dwellings, the oldest semi-civilization of the Western Continent. These people are supposed to have lived many hundreds of years before the Columbian discovery, and were remarkable not only for the vessels, cloths and mattings which they wove from blades of the alfalfa plant, the effective utensils and weapons which they wrought from bone, stone and wood, but particularly for their strange habitations, that were built of hewn stone in recesses of what appear to be inaccessible cliffs. The dwellings shown were reproductions made by the H. Jay Smith Exploring Co. of those that are still to be seen at frequent intervals along the Rio Mancos Cañon, of Colorado, and so skilfully arranged that the visitor to the display seemed to be standing in the very midst of the real ruins, and shaking hands, as it were, with the dusty remains of a people who played their part in the drama of the world more than a thousand years ago.

CALIFORNIA'S STATUE OF JAMES MARSHALL.—California's building was not only the second largest State structure on the Exposition Grounds, but among her beautiful, valuable and varied exhibits were several very interesting pieces of statuary, and other features of great attractiveness. Our photograph here printed is a splendid view of the heroic figure of James W. Marshall, whose name and fame are dear to all Californians as the first discoverer of gold in that auriferous commonwealth. The statue is an excellent likeness of that brave pioneer, and represents him as he is supposed to have appeared upon finding the first gold nugget at Sutter's mill, on January 19, 1848. He holds the golden chunk in his right hand and with his left points toward the spot in the stream where he found it. The original nugget is still preserved, and is the property of Judge W. W. Allen, of San Francisco.

GRAND LOGGIA OF MACHINERY BUILDING.—The architects of Machinery Building, or the Palace of Mechanical Arts, as it more properly should be called, were unable for a long while to conceive a design that would harmonize with the surrounding buildings and Court of Honor, and yet exhibit sufficient contrast and originality to accentuate its splendid features. They at length adopted the Spanish Renaissance style, which permitted the construction of a colonnaded façade, and made a loggia the full length of the building, 842 feet. What a glorious promenade this long avenue afforded, and what a view was there looking down the stretch of columnated gallery, which in the distance appeared to be a walled passageway of interminable length! From this immense colonnade, which was protected by a balustrade visitors had a commanding view of Administration Building and the Great Fountain, and were sufficiently near the music stand to hear the concerts while being entertained by the incomparable beauties of their surroundings.

THE NORWAY BUILDING.—A very curious structure was the Norway Government Building, with its cross-gables, and sharp peaks crowned with dragon heads. The architecture was that of the tenth and eleventh centuries, when the Vikings ruled the northern seas, and was intended to typify the period in which the Norsemen discovered and occupied America. The building was 25 x 60 and framed so that it could be easily taken apart. It was built in Christiana, and for a time was open to the inspection of those who were sufficiently interested in Norway's representation at the World's Fair to visit it. After services of dedication in Norway the building was taken apart and shipped to the Exposition grounds, where it was set up next to the Swedish Building. Our photograph gives an excellent view of the structure.

MANUFACTURES BUILDING AND WOODED ISLAND.—The view herewith shows the west side and north front of Manufactures Building, and also presents a splendid picture of Wooded Island, for as it is a winter scene the trees are shorn of their foliage, leaving the walks distinctly in view. The circular structure partly shown in the foreground is the White Star Steamship Company's Building, in which was exhibited a complete model of one of the finest steamers of their fleet. The magnitude and architectural proportions of Manufactures Hall are excellently and clearly exhibited in the photograph, and the detail of the bridge crossing the lagoon is likewise distinctly seen, as are the deer which ornament the piers of the west approach. The picture is one of the most comprehensive that was made at the Fair.

THE GREAT BELGIAN VASE.—Next to the French section in Manufactures Building was the Belgian Pavilion, in which there was a marvelously rich and valuable display of products from Ghent, Brussels, Antwerp and Liège. In front of the entrance to Belgium's exhibit was a bronze statue, seven feet high, of Leonidas at Thermopylæ, by Graef, of Bruges. On the right of this spirited statue was a dainty statuette representing "Innocence Tormented by Love," and on the left was the giant bronze vase shown in the photograph. The figure-work on this piece was simple, being restricted to two female heads at the base of the handles which rose above the crown in a double curve. It was a chaste example of bronze, notable for its gracefulness rather than for its elaborate design, but did not fail to excite the admiring interest of those who are capable of estimating the value of such productions.

THE MINES AND MINING BUILDING.—Facing Administration Building on the north, and projecting its length of 700 feet along the side of Electrical Building, was the structure in which was housed the wonderfully valuable, varied and unique displays of all the minerals that lie hidden in the underground storehouses of the world. The south front of the building is shown in the accompanying photograph, extending along the plaza 350 feet, and exhibiting to good effect the chaste Italian Renaissance style of the structure. The roof was largely of glass, so as to afford light for the galleries which ran around the interior, upon which many of the lighter exhibits were placed. The value of the displays exceeded those made in any other building, being placed at $50,000,000. Here was to be seen a large number of Kaffirs digging for diamonds as they do in the Kimberly mines of South Africa, and cutting, polishing and mounting the precious stones. There was also gold in big nuggets, silver in large bars and splendid statues, and such a profusion of mineral wealth that it would seem all the poor of the world might be made rich by its distribution.

WEST PORTION OF THE UNITED STATES SECTION OF PAINTINGS.—In the section before us is a splendid reproduction of Julian Story's great painting, elsewhere noticed, entitled "M'lle De Sombreuil" (an episode of the French Revolution), illustrating the bravery of a wife defending her husband against the wild ravenings of a Jacobin mob. The conspicuous small picture near by is Mr. Moore's "Japanese Musicians." Other prominent paintings are "Sappho," by Mrs. Sewell, and "Mother and Child," by Brush. The large picture was Mr. Story's masterpiece, and as it was the largest, so was it the gem of the collection that hung upon the walls of this room, and was deservedly the object of universal admiration.

A PORTION OF THE EXHIBIT MADE BY AMERICAN ARTISTS.—A very handsome view is here given of a part of the exhibit made in the Art Hall by American artists, whose work compared favorably in general, and exceeded in merit in many instances, with the works shown by the best foreign artists. The pictures distinguished in the above photograph are as follows: The large centre painting is by Blashfield, and is entitled "Christmas Bells;" on the right is Norton's "Return of the Herring Fleet," and below it on the right is a very pretty picture by Nettleton, called "Watching for the Return of the Fishermen;" on the extreme left is a piece of Mr. Reinhardt's work, entitled "Washed Ashore." Other paintings shown are, "Good Friday," by Elizabeth Nourse; "Road to the Village," by Metcalf, and "The Hour of Prayer," by Richards.

PERFORMANCE IN THE JAVANESE THEATRE.—A very beautiful interior view of the Javanese theatre is here presented, exhibiting the actors and actresses as they appeared on the stage. It is a peculiarity of Oriental theatres that the entire stage is always exposed, as there is no drop curtain, and the orchestra occupies a position which interferes at times with the free movement of the performers. The Javanese are great lovers of theatrical amusement, and some of the professionals display considerable ability as pantomimists, for actors never speak while on the stage. The female performers often have the merit of being very beautiful, and there were at least two in the company at the Fair that had this desirable qualification of actresses in a high degree. The performances consisted of pantomime drama and marionette exhibitions, the latter being very amusing, but the former were so tiresome that a short while sufficed to satisfy the curiosity of spectators.

THE JAVANESE VILLAGE.—The most interesting, though the smallest, people from foreign lands that came to the World's Fair were the Javanese, who, numbering thirty persons, built one of their characteristic bamboo villages on the north side of the Plaisance. The space allotted to them was some four acres, which was enclosed by a curious but deftly wrought bamboo fence twelve feet high. Within this area they erected living houses, and also a large theatre, all of bamboo, and covered them with palmetto thatch brought from their far away island home. The houses, as will be noticed by the photograph, were built upon piling, in accordance with the custom which universally prevails in Java, adopted as a provision against snakes and other unpleasant reptiles which abound on that island, and also against floods, which, in the rainy season, sweep all the level places like a deluge. The people are very mild mannered, small of stature, and as musical as they are industrious and frugal. The village every night resounded with the clash of cymbals, the rather strident voices of singers, and the soft and pleasant thrumming of the ongloong, a reed instrument somewhat resembling the xylophone, but more melodious.

GERMAN SECTION OF THE ART GALLERY.—German artists were represented at the Fair by some of the finest products of the brush of modern times. The display, too, large, consisting of nearly five hundred paintings. Our photograph represents Gallery Thirty-six of the German Section, showing the following pictures by celebrated artists: "Pets of Peasant's Wife," the work of Braith; "The Battle is Over," one of Boddien's productions; "The Swedish Coast," by Eschke; "H. M. S. Deutchland," by Hoecker; "Portrait of Hemhol by Knaus; "Landscape From the Harz," by Nabert; "After Bathing," by Ritter; "Battle of Stoezlk," Poland, 1831, by Rosen; "Emperor William II. Whaling on Board the *Duncan Gr* by Saltzmann; "Parade in Presence of the Emperor," by Schmidt; "Emperor William II.," by Schuch. There was an air of elegance and comfort in this gallery, where easy cushion s were provided for visitors, in marked contrast with the lack of resting places in many other rooms.

ENTRANCE TO THE LAPLAND VILLAGE.—Midway Plaisance was a scene of marvelous diversity, where the eye of curiosity was meeting with constant surprise, and where timid people were often thrown into a state of nervousness by startling announcement, and the sudden appearance of Cannibal, Indian, Fakir or Blue Beard. It was a wondrous melange in which the fierce character of every fairy tale might be seen, armed, savage, and insatiate. Among this olla podrida of uncivilized or semi-barbarous humanity, were the Lapland Villagers, a quiet but brave people, who came out of their icy country across the sea to become a par of the ethnological exhibition. The Laps are wild mannered and given to keeping in-doors, so the managers of the village had the contract on their hands of drawing visitors' attention to the Lapland show. Our picture shows the entrance, before which the noisy crier is exhorting visiting crowds to buy admission tickets to the village, promising all manner of interesting entertainment inside.

PERSIAN SWORDSMEN IN A MOCK DUEL.—The wonderful skill with which some of the Persians at the Fair handled the sword attracted large crowds to their daily exhibitions. Our picture represents two of them fighting a mock duel in which the principals rest on one knee before a referee. It was truly astonishing how viciously they slashed and thrust at each other without doing serious injury, but every stab and stroke was caught with marvellous dexterity on a small shield of hippopotamus-hide, which was their only guard. Possibly every movement was known beforehand, through long practice, like two clog-dancers who by training regulate the motions of their feet so perfectly that they dance as one man. But, however it was done, the Persian swordsmen simulated a fierce fight and wrought spectators up to the highest pitch of excitement.

LEFT CENTRE SECTION OF FRENCH SCULPTURES.—There are two specially prominent sculpture groups shown in the above photograph, one of which is allegoric of the French Republic elsewhere described. The second conspicuous piece is one of Geoffroy's masterpieces, representing a tiger devouring an antelope, a striking, strong and remarkably natural production, which shows in every line the genius that created it. In the background on the right is Chopin's bronze figure of a Volunteer of 1776. Other pieces are Washington and Lafayette, in spirited pose and patriotic fraternity; the dancing muse; a woman playing with her child, by Leroux; a bacchante and Mercury, by Hannaux; and two or three other pieces shown and described in another photograph.

A WEST PERSPECTIVE OF THE GRAND BASIN.—Looking westward from the great arch of the Peristyle a noble scene was presented, as is shown by the photograph above. The Golden back of Liberty Statue filled the foreground and emphasized the attractions that spread out on either side until the view was arrested by MacMonnies' Fountain and the stately magnificent Administration Building. On the south shore we observe the spacious lawns and their wealth of statuary fronting Agricultural and Machinery Buildings, that in the receding distance gleam like palaces resplendent with all the arts that genius is able to conceive. Along the north shore the vista is no less imposing, tracing the receding loggia of Manufactures Hall and the dwarfing beauties of the Electrical Building, with a misty interception of playing fountains whose spray in the distance looks like little clouds rising from the basin. On the water, that danced by sunlight and by moonbeam, glided pretty crafts filled with excursionists, whose shout and laugh mingled with the music that floated back from the concert stand, adding happiness to the sublimity of the scene.

NORTH END OF THE FRENCH STATUARY EXHIBIT.—A general view, from the south gallery, is here pictured of the French section, in which are to be observed several familiar marble figures and also some of the largest plaster groups that were shown at the Exposition. Among the new pieces are "The Fisherman," "Labor," and Lemaire's exquisitely lovely marble statuette, "La Cigale," perhaps the daintiest figure in the entire collection. In the rear of the section, as here photographed, are Cain's life-size plasters of "A Lion Strangling a Crocodile," "Two Eagles Fighting over the Carcass of a Bear" and "A Rhinoceros Attacked by Tigers." These pieces commanded the greatest attention and excited the most profound admiration of every one that saw them.

A SECTION OF ITALIAN STATUARY.—Italy was very fully represented in Art Hall by the exhibition of works of all her greatest painters and sculptors. In the latter she was first of all the nations represented, the number of pieces of all kinds of sculpture displayed being as follows: Italy, 284; France, 258; United States, 148; Germany, 118, and Great Britain at the foot of the list with only fifty-three. Among the figures shown in the photograph can be distinguished: "Arianna," by Garibaldi; "Plaster cast of Burns' Monument," by Apolloni; "Model of Dante Monument," by Troubetskoy; "Angel of the Resurrection," by Bardi; "A Monk Reading," by Rota; "No More Slaves," by Civiletti, and "The Last of the Spartans," by Trentanove.

PROCTOR'S STATUE OF AN INDIAN.—A companion-piece to the Cowboy was Proctor's superb staff statue of a Sioux Indian, which stood on the east bank of the lagoon near the Mining Building. An indistinct view of the Cowboy is also shown in the above illustration, so that the relative positions of these two figures may be seen. The Indian is a much better piece of art than the Cowboy, having been completed under the immediate direction of Mr. Potter, whose conception of the former is also much stronger. Seen from a distance, however, the companion statues appear to be ideally perfect and full of spirit. Each one is also complementary of the other, for, as seen from the Mining Building, mutual surprise is portrayed by the poses of the figures, though the positions should have been reversed had it been the idea of Mr. Proctor to show the two betraying anxiety as to the purposes of each other. The model for the Indian was Red Cloud, a Sioux chief.

QUAY OF THE WEST LAGOON.—Our illustration presents a close view of the artificial shore line of the west lagoon, and a misty vision of Transportation and Mining Buildings in the distance. The quay was made of boards, over which staff was laid, giving the appearance of a marble water-front, while a granitoid coping, and low pillars capped with slabs of the same material, made a raised wall, some three feet higher than the walk. At intervals there were landings for the gondolas and electric launches, where broad flights of steps led down to the water's edge. The view from any point of the lagoon was very charming, and at night was exceedingly romantic. The combination of palatial buildings, artistic bridges, swift-speeding launches, and the measured dip of the gondolier's oar, was like a visit to Venice of the Doges, or an apparition of Carthage in the golden days of Dido and Æneas. In the fading distance loomed up the shimmering domes of giant structures, and the tall spires that drew fire from the sun, while the intervales were crowded with white façades and blooming flower-beds of gorgeous colors, making the panorama one of super-splendor.

WROUGHT-IRON FENCE ENCLOSING GERMANY'S EXHIBIT.—One of the most exquisite pieces of workmanship to be seen in Manufactures Hall was the Wrought-iron Fence before Germany's exhibit, as shown in the photograph, a section of which was 160 feet long, with three gates, each forty feet high, twenty-two feet wide, and weighing, with their elaborate top-ornamentations, twenty tons. These gates were flanked with towers, supported by Ionic pillars whose plinths were decorated with golden eagles. The bars of the centre gate were fantastically wrought in the most delicate tracery work, and the decorations at the top were imitative of a bouquet of flowers. The work was suggestive of the silversmith more than of the iron craftsman, but the whole was executed by three score of the most skillful artisans in iron at Frankfort-on-the-Main, the task occupying more than six months' time.

STATUE OF THE FRENCH REPUBLIC.—One of the most splendid pieces of bronze statuary that was on exhibition at the Columbian Exposition occupied a place in the French section in the east side of Manufactures Building. The piece was an allegoric representation of the French Republic, and was so perfect in detail as well as significant in pose, as to typify to the very life the achievements and aspirations of the French nation. The figure was that of Liberty voicing the rights of man, with a sword in the left hand, point downward, typical of the force in reserve to compel respect for the law whose *sine qua non* is fraternity, liberty and equality. The tablet in the left hand represented the ordinances of the Republic, which are protected by the aegis of the sword, which though unsheathed is Liberty's last resort. The central idea embodied in the statue, an idea which represents the fruits of all the struggles, the defeats no less than the triumphs, of the nation, is that eternal vigilance is not only the price of liberty, but equality before the law can be maintained only through the exercise of justice, and that justice is armed with the power to guard the rights of the weak, as well as to restrain the temper of the arrogant, the vicious, and the strong.

THE GREAT YERKES TELESCOPE.—The picture above presented is an excellent photographic view of the great Yerkes telescope as it appeared when mounted, ready for observations, at the north end of the main aisle in Manufactures Hall. Improvement in telescopes has been very great during the past twenty years, but it was thought that the completion of the thirty-six inch refracting instrument in Lick observatory marked the limit of perfect lenses, and that it was impossible to make a telescope of greater magnifying power. This prediction has been proven false by the construction of the great Yerkes instrument here shown. It has a lens that is forty inches in diameter, and has a focal length of thirty-five feet. This monster instrument was built by Warner & Swasey upon the order of Fred Yerkes, the street-car millionaire of Chicago, who made a gift of it to the **Chicago University.**

GRAEF'S STATUE OF LEONIDAS.—The Hero of Thermopylæ, the imperishable glory that made Sparta,—though it has disappeared from the map,—a country as memorable as history ever perpetuated, was never more grandly represented than by Graef, of quaint old Brueges, in his statue of Leonidas. This superb bronze figure, which was seven feet high, stood at the entrance to the Belgian Section in Manufactures Building. It is beautifully pictured in the photograph which is here presented. The statue is not that of the Spartan when he wrote the message-epitaph of himself and handful of followers, "Go, stranger, and tell at Lacedemon, etc.," but in the attitude of challenging the millions of Greek that Xerxes commanded, and as leading his brave hundred into the pass where glory and the grave awaited them.

REAR VIEW OF MACMONNIES' FOUNTAIN.—From whatever side the great MacMonnies', or Columbian Fountain was viewed, it presented a sight of extraordinary grandeur and artistic beauty. The fountains of Versailles are a trifle larger, but in point of splendor of design no other fountain in the world can be classed as its equal. In this respect it must be accepted as the most glorious conception of modern sculptors, notwithstanding its perishable nature. The near view here presented is from a point in front of Administration Building looking directly east, towards the Peristyle. Critical examination of the figures fails to show any neglect of execution as indicating the ephemeral character of the work, for the details are finished in the highest perfection. Old Father Time is life-like in every feature and lineament, and his attitude reflects the solemnity of his task. The nymph sporting with her children in the water is equally realistic, but in contrast faithfully exhibits her wantonness, thus bringing out the character of the main figures of the Barge more strikingly and impressively.

A SECTION OF ITALIAN PAINTINGS.—The photograph herewith presents a view of a portion of the Italian exhibit of oil paintings in Art Hall. The large marble figure in the foreground is "Eve, after Sin," by the famous Italian sculptor Allegretti. The bust to the right is Civilatti's "School-boy," and the bronze group on the left represents "An Arab's Family Traveling," the work of Biondi. The prominent pictures that can be distinguished, are as follows: "Boatman's Canal," by Bottero; "The First Born," by Bruenn; "Harvest of Indian Corn," by Carcani; "Declaration of Love," by Conconi; "Golden Dreams," by De Tommasi; "Eviction," by Gasperini, and "A Child of the Fields," by Savini.

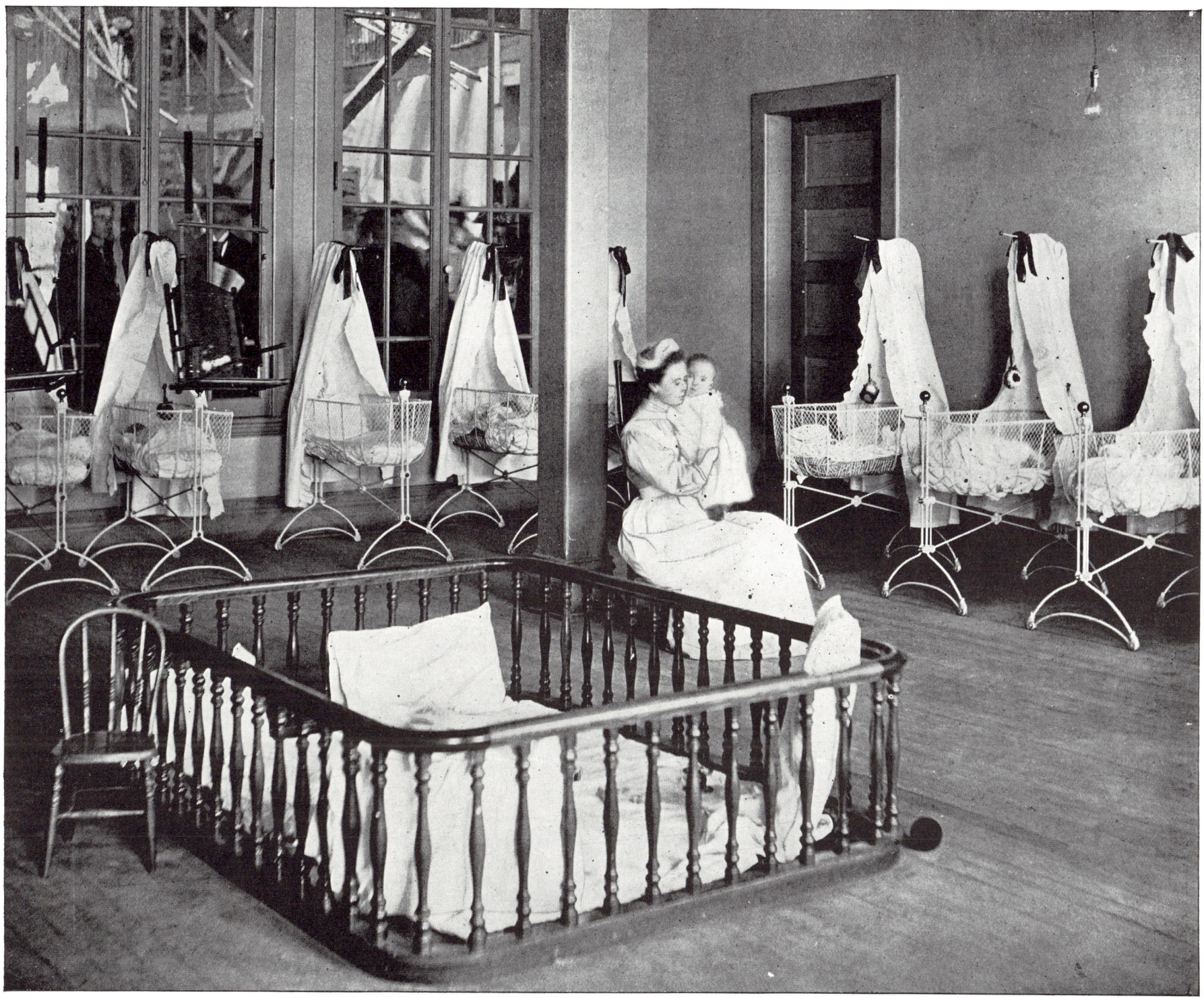

NURSERY IN THE WOMAN'S BUILDING.—The Board of Lady Managers, and their efficient and able assistants, whose efforts were so well directed and untiring, are entitled to the highest praise that can be bestowed for the splendid achievements of the sex at the Fair. The direction of their labors was towards the elevation of woman in all walks of life, and also in the better and most intelligent care of children. Our description of the Woman's Building, and the gymnasium therein, briefly told the story of what the spirited and highly intellectual ladies did at the Fair, exhibiting them as endowed with executive qualifications equal to that which the best of the sterner sex can boast; the above photograph illustrates the loving, motherly sentiment which was practically manifested by the lady managers in the provisions made by them for the care of infants at the Fair. The arrangements comprehended not only a model nursery presided over by trained nurses, but also a spacious play-room where children might be left in the care of faithful attendants by mothers visiting the Fair. It was an infants' check-room, a novel but most excellent provision appreciated by thousands of women.

EXHIBIT OF THE SOCIETY OF POLISH ARTISTS.—The pretty photograph herewith, represents a section of Group 140, containing an exhibition of oil paintings made by the Society of Polish Artists in the Art Palace. Among the pictures most easily distinguishable are Popiel's masterpiece, entitled, "After the Storm," a strong creation of a great artist; "Where Shall We Go?" by Kasiewicz; "A Moorish Girl," by Alchimowicz; "Harvest in Sandomir," by Pawlowski; and, "A Portrait," by Ciaglinski. Nearly all the works shown in the Polish gallery were subjects illustrating the national life, and many of them exhibited the longing desire of the people of that unhappy country for independence. Some of the pictures were too patriotic for exhibition in Russia, against which there is a deep Polish hatred.

THE CASINO.—Elsewhere in this series of World's Fair views is a photographic picture of the Peristyle and the flanking buildings, Music Hall on the north and the Casino on the south. Our present reproduction shows the latter building much more advantageously. A large reclamation from the lake was made by driving piling, upon which not only the pier, but the Casino, Peristyle, and Music Hall were erected as shown in the illustration. The size and exterior appearance of the Casino and Music Hall were identical, the structures being of Roman Renaissance style and each one, as well as the Peristyle, was surmounted with heroic figures representing the arts, science, drama and music.

PROCTOR'S STATUE OF LABOR.—On the north side of the Grand Basin, at a boat landing in front of Manufactures Building, stood the heroic statue shown above. It was one of Mr. Proctor's best figures, designed to represent "Labor," which the group and posing speakingly represent. The coatless and brawny man in the very prime of his strength, and the heavy-limbed and strong-muscled Norman horse in harness, chafing to be about his work, tell everything that the sculptor sought to convey by the figures. A similar group occupied a pedestal at the west end of the short flight of steps which led up from the boat landing.

GALLERY No. 9 OF THE UNITED STATES SECTION OF PAINTINGS.—The above is a very beautiful and clear view of one of the most interesting sections of United States exhibit of oil paintings. Only a few of the pictures are large, but they are all specimens from the brushes of the best artists of American nativity. Some of the paintings easily distinguishable are: "Lapping Waves on a Quiet Shore," by Bisbing; "Woman at the Mosque, Algiers," by Bridgman; "A Legend of the Desert," by Du Mond; "A Marine," by Harrison; "Site of Ancient Memphis," by Pope; and portraits by Sartain, Robbins, Putnam and Stewart.

THE GERMAN EXHIBIT OF ART MANUFACTURES.—It is hardly giving more credit than is due to say that the German exhibit of fine arts in Manufactures Building was one of the principal sights of the exhibition. The space asked for and allotted to Germany in this department (160 feet in length) was hardly so large as that used by some other nations, but the display made more than compensated for the rather limited area occupied. As shown by the photograph, the centre piece and wings of the section exhibit a wondrously rich embellishment of wood carving and statuary, in keeping with the resplendent showcases and cabinets that contained the art displays. In front of the centre piece was a basin and small *jet d'eau*, with figures of nymphs supporting a shell, on the top of which rested a dove carrying a cupid that was toying with a dainty water-pipe. Even amid this scene of artistic display the intense military spirit of Germany was represented by a bronze bust statue of a soldier, which was set upon a bracket attached to one of the spiral columns of the central cabinet. The exhibition of articles included specimens of the finest glassware, plaques, bronzes, vases and other *objects de vertu* almost without number, and of endless diversity.

MINNESOTA'S POMOLOGICAL EXHIBIT.—Our photograph above pictures a section of Minnesota's exhibit in Agricultural Building. The State made a splendid display of farm products for which she is famous, such as grains and grasses, but comparatively few outside of the State knew that her soil was so well adapted to the raising of fruits, as her pomological exhibit showed it to be. The view herewith shows a portion of the section which was assigned to Minnesota in which to expose samples of the large and splendid apples that her great orchards yield; also fine peaches, grapes and other products which she is producing for the world's markets. The display here shown was made by the Minnesota State Horticultural Society.

THE SCULPTURED CROWN OF THE PERISTYLE.—Next to MacMonnies' Fountain, the most beautiful sculpture work seen at the Exposition, is that admirably shown in the above photograph. The arched passage which pierces the Peristyle was called the Watergate, emblematic of the gateway to the New World. In carrying out this allegory the architect provided for the figures which ornamented the Colonnade and the Crown of the Peristyle. The large group on the summit represented the triumph of Columbus and symbolized his glorious discovery. The cornice was likewise a memorial of the early explorers, and bore the names of Ponce de Leon, De Soto, Champlain, La Salle and Cortez. Large-sized figures representing types of American races were placed on the anchors of the balustrade, and appropriate lines were inscribed on the Crown of the Watergate. This magnificent creation of architect and sculptor was completely destroyed by fire on the night of January 8, 1894.

NORTH COURT OF UNITED STATES SCULPTURE EXHIBIT.—In the charming photograph above we have an advantageous view of a small portion of the statuary exhibits that were arranged in the north court of the United States section. The strongest piece, perhaps, in the exhibition is Daniel French's bas-relief plaster, entitled "Death and the Sculptor;" next to that, on the right, is a statue by Bartlett, representing the "Ghost Dance," and "A Tiger at Bay," also a plaster, by Peterson. On the right are four very beautiful marbles: "The Fisherman's Daughter," by Turner; "Diana Reclining," by Warner; "A Nubian Captive," by Griffith; and "Evening," by Ruckstuhl.

UNITED STATES SCULPTURE IN THE ROTUNDA OF ART PALACE.—The grand, heroic and life-like statue which is the chief object in the above photograph is one of the best-known figures of Washington that was ever made. It has been illustrated in a hundred historical works, and is regarded as a typical likeness of our greatest countryman. The statue is a bronze, by Thomas Ball, and was lent by E. F. Searles, of Massachusetts. The lovely marble group on the left is entitled "Diana and the Lion," a front view of which is shown in another photograph in the series; it was sculptured by Elwell. The group on the left is called "Shipwrecked," and was shown and described in a previous number. In the rear are to be seen "A Cavalryman in Campaigning Dress," a plaster; and next to it is a bronze figure representing "A Frolicsome Boy"—both the work of Astanieres.

PANORAMA OF THE NORTHWEST LAGOON.—A romantic, dreamy, idyllic view is here presented—the appearance of a lake embowered with profusion of delicate vegetation set in the midst of a city of magic splendor. Along the sedgy edges of the lagoon are nesting places of waterfowls, and the old fishing boat is suggestive of a retreat little disturbed by the throng of World's Fair visitors. But across the placid water are to be seen the gleaming wonders of architecture that brought the great Exposition into everlasting fame. Toward the north towers the capitoline dome of Illinois Building, and crowding the left bank are to be seen the massive dome of Horticultural Building emphasizing the beauty of the association of splendid structures. The view is picturesquely charming, as it is wondrously diversified by remarkable contrasts.

PENNSYLVANIA'S BUILDING.—Opposite the north front of the Art Palace and adjacent to New York, its sister commonwealth, was Pennsylvania's Building, one of the grandest structures on the grounds. The front, as will be noticed, is a copy of Independence Hall, and was built of brick instead of the perishable material used in the construction of nearly all the other State buildings. It had spacious verandas and wide porches for the comfort of visitors, and besides being a really splendid structure, was beautified by pieces of magnificent allegoric statuary. On the two corners shown in the photographs were groups representing respectively "Mines and Manufactures," and "The Arts and Sciences." Above the front entrance pediment was a beautiful statuary coat of arms of the State, and on either side of this were statues of the two most famous men identified with Pennsylvania's history, Penn and Franklin. The interior of the building was finished in native woods and marble, and the furnishing was very fine. At the main doorway was placed the Old Liberty Bell, that attracted the almost reverent attention of all who entered the building. The dimensions of the structure were 110 x 166 feet, and the cost was $60,000.

THE SWEDISH GOVERNMENT BUILDING.—Queen Sophie, of Sweden, took such a lively interest in the World's Fair that she enlisted the co-operation not only of her government, but also of the most distinguished persons in the Swedish Empire, and especially the first ladies in her country. It was, therefore, largely through her Majesty's efforts that the splendid Swedish Government Building was erected and filled with a choice collection of art and manufactures made by artists and artisans of that nation.

The building, the main front of which is pictured above, occupied a triangular space of 100 x 200 feet near the north line of Fisheries Building. Its designer was Gustavus Wickman, of Stockholm, who adopted for his model a style which was somewhat common in the sixteenth century. All the frame work of the building was made in Sweden and temporarily put together there to afford the people a view of it, after which it was taken to pieces and sent to this country, together with a sufficient quantity of brick, terra-cotta and cement to make the front wall of the first story, and thus to give the building a more substantial appearance. The central section terminated in a high dome and steeple, in which latter a bell was hung after the custom of the time, and was colored in a most pleasing fashion so as to catch the eye as it wandered over the grounds.

MAIN ENTRANCE OF THE WOMAN'S BUILDING.—The Woman's Building was located amid especially picturesque surroundings. Immediately in front the lagoon broadened to 400 feet, with a landing at a stone stairway which led up to a terrace 100 feet broad beflowered with blooming shrubbery and beds of flaming colors. The building was of Italian renaissance style, but the central entrance was an approach to the Greek Ionic. The first story was elevated ten feet from the ground, and was reached by a broad flight of stone steps through a triple arched colonnade. Directly over the main entrance was another open colonnade and promenade, to which three doors gave access. The columns were of Corinthian style with finely carved capitals supporting an entablature and frieze that was decorated with wreaths in relief. But it was in the pediment that the richest and most pretentious sculpture work was shown, being composed of groups of female figures illustrative of woman's responsibilities, and a central figure representing justice holding the book of human rights and just ordinances in her hand.

THE JAVANESE THEATRE.—Our view of the Javanese theatre was taken two months before the Exposition opened, when a light snow lay upon the palm leaf roof of the building, in strong contrast with the airiness of a structure suggestive of a tropical climate. The interior was sparsely furnished, with common chairs on a very slightly inclined floor, and a plain stage destitute of such accessories as wings, scenery or drop curtain. There were 125 natives, of whom thirty-six were women, in the village, and of this number nearly one-fourth took part from time to time in the performances. The show—for it was a show more than a performance—was a sort of pantomime, in which the movements of the actors were explained by an interpreter. A native orchestra, called a gamelan, composed of twenty-four men, made a rather harmonious noise on queer instruments, to which dancing girls responded in gyrations that had little in them of graceful motion. As a show, however, the Java theatre was a great attraction, as a sight of the natives satisfied curiosity.

A GROUP OF GONDOLIERS.—The attention of boat-riding visitors at the World's Fair was divided between the gondolas and the electric launches, the former being generally preferred by ladies, by reason of the romantic interest with which they are invested. The lagoon, winding its way like a silvered avenue between beautiful buildings, was typical of the water-streets of Venice, crowded with swift-speeding boats laden with pleasure parties. At night the scene was still more poetic, the gleam of rippling water catching the reflections of moonbeam or electric lights, the soft splash of oar, the guitar's music, and songs of merry girls and boys, was like a dream or poem of the "City of the Sea." Our photograph represents a party of gondoliers brought direct from Venice to the Magic City by the lake, and who propelled their pretty boats through the sinuous lagoons during the season of the Exposition.

A BEDOUIN WOMAN FROM SYRIA.—It was not until very recent years that any member of the Syriac tribe of Bedouins visited this country, and no woman of that strange people ever saw America until the Columbian Exposition opened, and attracted, through shrewd show managers, a company of genuine nomadic Syrians. The woman whose picture is here given belonged to the Aneze sub-division of the Bedouin tribe, the most numerous and powerful of the fierce Arab nomads, who levy tributes upon caravans and travelers, fearless of the Turkish government, to which they acknowledge only the shadow of allegiance. The people to whom the woman belongs are a mixture of pure Arabic and Gypsy blood; they are Mohammedans in faith, polygamous in custom, and bandits by instinct, with nothing better to recommend them than the contra virtue of cunning and dashing bravery. The woman is shown in her characteristic dress, which consists of a loose, long, flowing garment caught at the waist by a girdle of the same material, and a semi turban that hides the hair and nearly all the forehead. For ornaments she wears disks of tin as shown in the illustration.

THE DOUBLE GHABEET, OR WEDDING SADDLE, OF THE ARABS.—There was great curiosity excited in those who visited the Arab Village at the Fair by an exhibition of a camel specially caparisoned for a bride and groom, photograph of which is here given. In Arabia, Persia, Syria and Turkestan the camel is an indispensable beast. From his hair the finest fabrics are woven, the flesh is used extensively for food, though most unpalatable to an untrained taste, and camel's milk is said to be a delicious and very nutritive drink. But it is as a beast of burden that the dromedary especially is most valuable. He can travel at a speed of six miles per hour for fifteen hours out of twenty-four for a week; can do without water for a week in summer; can live off anything, whether it be thorns, cactus or dry grass, and can easily carry a load of 400 pounds. For these virtues he gets no reward, scarcely a shelter to protect him from the storms, or a grain of corn from his master's granary. He is put to all manner of uses to which a carrying animal is amenable, and one of these uses is serving as a means of transportation for bridal couples. In nearly all Oriental countries weddings are affairs of small consequence, since they are practically contracted in infancy. Women are rarely seen and never heard; so when a couple are wed and go upon a bridal trip they use a camel instead of a railroad or a steamboat. The bride and groom take seats in a double Ghabeet, or canopied saddle, as shown in the illustration, and thus hidden from view, and without exchanging a word, proceed solemnly to their destination.

A PERSIAN DRESS=PARADE SOLDIER.—The photograph herewith represents a Persian in the military costume of an officer, his long recurved sword being the weapon which is worn by officers in that country upon all occasions. It is not an affected position which the subject has taken, for the Persians are, as they have been for centuries, noted for their habit of reclining whenever they are not actively engaged. When one Persian makes a social call upon another he is invited to recline with his host upon a divan or rich carpet. And even when eating, it is the custom to recline in the position shown in the above illustration, and to permit this position to all persons while dining the table is set in the shape of a U, around the three sides of which the guests recline on richly upholstered and thickly padded benches, and use their hands unassisted by knives and forks.

A JAVANESE BRIDE AND GROOM.—From the far-away East Indies, from the tropics of the great islands of the Pacific, which Columbus set out to reach when arrested in his course by the New World, came tawny-skinned people to the Columbian Fair. Among these islanders were a number of Javanese, samples of the Malayan race, who have a history most ancient and wonderful. Their religion is ostensibly Mohammedanism but it is the religion of conquest rather than of faith, for they generally entertain the beliefs inherited from their remote ancestors, which is polytheistic and Shamanistic, of witchcraft and diabolism. Their customs are peculiar as their beliefs, but differ essentially from those of the Singalese and their northern neighbors, with whom they hold commercial intercourse. Marriage with them is only a convenience, and polygamy is not uncommon. Early marriages are encouraged, and the age at which contracts are usually made is when the boy reaches fourteen and the girl twelve. Such a marriage took place between a Javanese couple of these years at their village in the Midway Plaisance, and was celebrated in an imposing manner. A photograph of this young couple, taken a few days after their alliance, is given above.

THE BEAUTIFUL AGRICULTURAL BUILDING.—The United States, while rapidly increasing its manufacturing interests, is still most largely an agricultural nation, and as a recognition of this superior industry the Great Agricultural Building was erected, a magnificent picture of which is here presented. This wondrous edifice was 800 feet long and 500 feet in width, with a floor space of nineteen acres, and though practically a single-story structure the cost was $618,000. The architecture, however, showed heroic treatment, and its ornamentation was more elaborate than that of any other large building ever constructed. The main entrance was 64 feet wide, commanded by Corinthian pillars 50 feet high, and from the rotunda rose a spacious dome 100 feet in diameter covered with glass that lighted the interior in day time. A large loggia surrounded the building, and in the main vestibule were splendid pieces of statuary typifying agriculture. Indeed, there were scores of statues and pieces of sculpture, many of which are elsewhere particularly described.

PICTURESQUE TYPES OF THE MIDWAY.—In this gallery of the Plaisance characters we have portraits of a Syrian swordsman; a Moorish lady; an Egyptian donkey driver; a Bulgarian gentleman; a Javanese girl, and a boy from Upper Egypt.

TYPES OF ALL NATIONS IN THE PLAISANCE.—Nearly all of the characters above pictured are described elsewhere in this serial. The types herewith are as follows: An Egyptian boy; a fair Persian; a Bedouin; an Arab; Moorish dancing girls; and a Norwegian maid that attracted so many admirers in the Scandinavian café.

THE GREAT ALLIS ENGINE.—One of the sights in Machinery Hall was the colossal Allis engine, that supplied a greater part of the power used in driving the machinery within the building. The power was applied chiefly to two enormous dynamos, from which it was transmitted to smaller dynamos and shafting. In this transmission two seventy-two-inch belts were used, each of which drove a Westinghouse dynamo capable of developing 15,000 lights. Near by were other dynamos gaining their power from the same source and developing a total of 158,000 lights. These transmitted a current through a switch-board two stories high and seventy-eight feet long, thence leading by cables running through a fire-proof subway to all the buildings on the ground, providing power for the magnificent illuminations that made nights at the Fair so glorious.

INTERIOR VIEW OF ELECTRIC BUILDING.—A more wonderful, magical sight was never seen than that revealed by the marvelous displays of electrical apparatus, machinery and devices made in the Electric Building, the large central nave of which is herewith shown. In the foreground, at the left, are to be seen great electric lenses used in lighthouses; a little beyond these is the Westinghouse pavilion, and next in the rear is the Edison section, beyond which is the Edison electric column, covered with five thousand electric globes. Beautiful as was the scene in daytime, the vast theatre of electric wonders was robed with a magical splendor at night, which made it infinitely more gorgeous. It was a hall of marvels, a museum of enchantments, where the eye of curiosity was almost blinded by bewilderment and dazzled by surprises. No pen can ever describe the matchless illumination of that fairy-like exhibition, or fittingly picture the glories of the displays. Fortunately, our photograph preserves at least a daylight view of the general appearance of the hall and the wonderful exhibits therein.

OTHER TYPES OF THE MIDWAY.—The ethnologist might have gone no further than the Columbian Fair to find the races of the world and practically study their characteristics, for it was the assembling place of a remarkable variety, all of whom are pictured in this serial. The types above are: A girl from the Himalayan country; a Corean young man and girl; an Egyptian donkey boy; an Indian scout; two young Javanese girls, and a Mexican dandy.

A PROCESSION OF THE NATIONS.—Passing before the wondering eyes of Fair visitors, along the Plaisance, was a remarkable vision, comprehending nearly every semi-civilized type of the world. The photographs herewith include a Turkish athlete, the Corean Commissioner, a Javanese actress, a girl from Johore, two Corean girls, and a Turkish gentleman.

ROTUNDA OF THE FINE ART PALACE.—The photograph here presented is another and more extensive view of the United States exhibit of sculpture, in the rotunda of Fine Art Hall. Some of the figures are shown, from other points of observation, in previous views, but the principal statue—excepting that of Washington—here seen was not included among the statuary shown in other photographs of the same section in this serial. The strikingly beautiful life-size marble figure in the left foreground is "Christ and the Little Child," by Ball, the sculptor who modeled the heroic bronze statue of Washington. It is an exquisite piece, ranking with Rodolpho Bernardelli's marble of "Christ and the Adulteress," to which it ought to be a companion. To the left of this group is seen, distantly, a figure representing "Young Sophocles leading the chorus of Victory after the battle of Salamis." On the right are statues of Pan, Hercules, model for a Caryatid, and Diana and the Lion.

DOOR AND GALLERY OF THE LIMOGES CATHEDRAL.—A beautiful and classical work is the architecture and carving of the door to the Cathedral of Limoges, a reproduction of which was shown in the Art Palace, French section. The building was a sixteenth century structure, extremely elegant, as characterized the architecture of churches and public buildings of that period. On the left is a beautiful marble group by Magnier, representing "A Nymph and Cupid." In front of the doorway is a statue of "A Shepherd and Little Satyr," by Coysevox. The sculptor who reproduced in plaster the door and façade shown in the photograph, was Pierrie. In the foreground is a vase of the seventeenth century modeled by Lehongre.

CHARACTERS IN THE MIDWAY.—The several types represented in the above illustrations are: a Persian; Algerian chief and girls; a Hindostanee; a Turk; group of Egyptians, and a girl that danced at the Eiffel Tower Exhibition.

THE MIDWAY CONGRESS OF RACES.—Other representatives of Oriental peoples are pictured above as follows: The Hungarian Quartette, that sang in the Moorish Theatre; a Singhalese man, wife and daughter; a Javanese family; two girls from India; a Buddhist representative to the Congress of Religions; and a Corean father and son.

DOORWAY OF THE CATHEDRAL OF BORDEAUX.—Elsewhere in this serial is a photograph showing a three-quarter view of this splendidly sculptured doorway of the west façade of the Bordeaux Cathedral, and also some of the effigies and statues adjacent. Immediately in front is the beautiful marble tomb of Francis II., finely carved and covered with allegoric figures typical of the rigorous life and heavenly aspiration of that French ruler, husband of the beautiful but unfortunate Mary, Queen of Scots. On the right is a statue entitled "A Hamadryad and Child," and on the left a companion figure representing "The Garonne River," both the work of Coysevox.

AN AVENUE IN MACHINERY HALL.—A charming perspective scene is herewith presented, affording an elegant view of the central avenue of Machinery Hall, extending a length of nearly 1000 feet. In this great building was a marvelous exhibit of the most perfect machinery ever devised by the genius of man, performing work with what seemed to be the highest intelligence, and exciting the amazement of visitors whichever way they turned to make their examinations. There were machines at work turning out needles, pins, buttons, thimbles, and such small articles as are very cheap and common, but which everybody wonders how they are produced. In other sections were giant trip-hammers pounding with the most tremendous force, and yet as responsive to the touch of an operator as the most delicate instrument. Here all nations presented respectively specimens of the finest and most perfect machinery invented by their subjects, and the exhibition was thus the grandest of the kind ever made.

A REMARKABLE DIVERSITY OF NATIONALITIES.—A visit to the Midway was like a trip around the world, introducing as it did representatives of nearly every nation. The types photographed above, are: A Javanese girl, plump and pretty; an Algerian girl; a girl from Nazareth; a Japanese lady; a Moorish ballet girl; and an old lady who distinguished herself by walking all the way from New York to Chicago, to attend the Fair.

A MAGNIFICENT PICTURE OF INTERIOR OF AGRICULTURAL HALL.—One of the most comprehensive photographic views that was taken of the interior of any World's Fair building is herewith presented. While it does not afford a particular sight, in detail, of any single exhibit, the picture reveals at one expansive glance the general appearance of nearly the whole interior of that stupendous hall, in which was gathered the grandest, as it was the largest, collection of farm products that the human eye ever looked upon. Distinct photographs of particular exhibits will be found elsewhere in this serial, but beautiful as they are, no other can equal the impressive, comprehensive and charming view of the colossal hall that is here shown.

NORTH VIEW, BETWEEN ELECTRICITY AND MANUFACTURES BUILDING.—The point of observation from which the above photograph was taken was the northwest corner of Agricultural Building, looking across the plaza in front of that structure, and the Grand Basin. The view is a very pleasing one, exposing as it does the whole east front of Electricity Building, extending its 600 feet of length along the east lagoon, and the two beautiful bridges that afforded passage to Manufactures Hall, directly from the north and south ends of the former. Away beyond, indicating in a measure the great extent of the Fair Grounds, are to be seen the tops of some of the large buildings in the northern section, the whole embracing a charming panorama that suggests a city of incomparable splendor, such as indeed it was.

CENTRE OF THE FRENCH STATUARY SECTION.—Several of the figures to be seen in the accompanying photograph will be recognized in other pictures of the series, but though the statues are repeated the views are taken from different positions and are beautiful enough to justify their presentation in other illustrations. The statuary pieces most easily distinguished are "Aurora," by Michel; "Fox," a pointer, by Fougues; "The Blind Man and the Paralytic," by Michel; "The First Born," by Levasseur; "Nymph Echo," by Goudez; "A Volunteer Soldier of 1776," by Choppin; "Joan of Arc," by Chapu; "Man of the Stone Age," by Fremiet; and a foreshortened figure on the square pedestal in the foreground, of "The Martyr St. Catherine," by Pompon.

THE HO-O-DEN, OR PHŒNIX BIRD BUILDING ERECTED BY JAPAN.—The Japanese are too closely identified with their very close Chinese neighbors to be free from the gruesome superstitions which particularly distinguish the latter people; but it was with some surprise the Fair officials learned that the space allotted to Japan would be occupied by a building imitative of the most famous temple on that island, at Kioto, which was erected some centuries ago to perpetuate a remarkable fable. For the construction of an imitation of the Phœnix Bird Temple on Wooded Island, the Mikado contributed $50,000 from his private fortune, and sent over Japanese carpenters to do the work under the direction of Mr. Tegima, the Commissioner. The building was finished in May, 1892, and presented to Chicago, so that it will remain a permanent feature of Jackson Park, but rather as a curiosity than as a beautiful addition to the Park attractions. The original Temple is said to be the most charming structure in Japan, but if so the country cannot justly lay claim to being architecturally magnificent.

SANTA MARIA, THE FLAGSHIP OF COLUMBUS.—The object of supreme interest at the Great Exposition was unquestionably the replica of Columbus' flagship, the Santa Maria, which came across the Atlantic as the gift of Spain, to revive and illustrate the glorious achievement of the first Admiral of the Western Sea. This vessel of the past, a counterfeit relic of the middle ages, a cumbersome carack of the days of chivalry, sailed out of the harbor of antiquity in full life of the long ago, from the Old World to the New, wafted by the blessings and benedictions of Providence. The Santa Maria was built by the Spanish government after designs submitted by the most learned archeologists, and is an exact reproduction in every detail of construction and equipment of Columbus' flagship. Her dimensions are 63 feet over all, 20 feet beam, and 10½ feet depth of hold. She sailed out of Palos harbor in February, 1893, and arrived safely, under escort of the Bennington, at Hampton Roads, April 21 following. Thence she proceeded to Chicago, by way of the St. Lawrence River and the Great Lakes, manned by a Spanish crew who remained on her until the close of the Exposition.

THE WHITE HORSE INN.—One of the very interesting buildings situated in the north end of the Fair grounds is that so admirably shown in the photograph printed above. It acquired great reputation by reason of the fact that the building was an exact reproduction, both in size and construction, of an old country inn at Ipswich, England, immortalized by Dickens in his famous Pickwick papers. In the gabled balcony room shown in the left end of the building, is where Pickwick is fabled to have had his adventure with the old maid. And other rooms were pointed out as the places where similar apocryphal escapades occurred described by the great novelist. The original building is very old, its history dating back certainly as far as 1450. The reproduction was used at the Fair as a restaurant, where the cooking and service was severely English, and where the bar was attended by genuine English bar-maids.

THE JOHORE BUNGALOW VILLAGE.—The Malay Peninsula, a narrow strip of land separated from the island of Sumatra by the Malacca Straits, and whose metropolis is Singapore, was represented at the World's Fair by commissioners appointed by the Sultan of Johore, and made a very creditable showing. The exhibits from that remote land were made in the Agricultural Building, but besides these there was a bungalow—or native house of thatch and boards—village on the Midway, photograph of which is here shown. Johore being quite near to Sumatra and Java, and its merchants trading extensively with the natives of those islands, there are many similar characteristics between the two peoples in dress, customs, and the architecture of their buildings, though the Johoreans dominate, through their quick intelligence, great courage, and immense wealth. The houses, as will be seen, have the characteristic peculiar to the East India region bordering the sea, of being considerably elevated, and also in the general use of bamboo and palm leaves for roofing. The bungalow village was not an object of much interest, and comparatively few persons visited it.

REPRESENTATIVES OF THE DAHOMIAN CANNIBALS.—In another part of this series of World's Fair photographs is a description of the more remarkable and characteristic customs of the Dahomey cannibals. The picture herewith exhibits two of these representatives who have begun to adapt themselves to the new conditions of their American surroundings. In Dahomey the climate is tropical, so that clothing is unnecessary, save as a badge of semi-decency, but the Dahomians were not long on exhibition at the Midway Village before they developed a pride to imitate their visitors. Accordingly, we observe the two specimens above, habited in a conglomerate raiment of old coat and the American flag as a distinction of the male sex, and a cast-off dress, parti-colored with patches, and split so as to admit of its being worn *negligé*, distinguishing the female. They also picked up several expressions, among which a request for "Chicago beer" was most frequently used in their limited conversation with visitors; but when the pinching weather of October winds and frost attacked their bare limbs the Dahomians lost interest in everything except desire to return to their native country.

GERMAN EDUCATIONAL EXHIBIT.—The photograph here presented represents the display made by the "Berlin Society for the Education of the People." Pestalozzi is dear to the world as the author of the objective method of imparting instruction, who converted his own home into an orphan asylum and began teaching the inmates by object lessons, which proved so successful that his method soon became known and is now used in nearly every school in Europe. Froebel is distinguished as the author of the kindergarten system, and the memory of these two great German educators is sacredly preserved, as is illustrated by the monumental character of the educational display made in the Liberal Arts Building, by the Berlin Society.

ONE OF THE GREAT ENGINES IN MACHINERY BUILDING.—The largest electric generator that was ever built was that of the General Electric Company, with a capacity of 3000 horse-power, and costing $100,000. Next to this monster was the Allis Engine, photograph of which is shown above. This enormous piece of machinery weighed 325 tons, and in its thirty-ton cylinder a man six feet tall could walk without stooping. The belts that ran on its two pulley wheels were each six feet wide, and the power it exerted was equal to 2000 horses. To move this iron giant a special traveling crane had to be built, the track of which may be seen in the photograph.

THE GREATEST LOCOMOTIVE IN ENGLAND.—The mighty "Lord of the Isles" deserves a palace and a long rest, for it was in service for forty years, and for half that time wore the honors of being the fastest engine in England. It was exhibited at the London Fair of 1851, and drew admiration from every one for the speed with which it had daily covered the distance between London and Bath, the rate often exceeding sixty miles per hour. This was a marvelous speed twenty-five years ago, but the New York Central Railroad exhibited the famous engine No. 999, which for a short spurt ran at a speed of 112 miles per hour, and which makes 90 and 100 miles, for short distances, nearly every day. "Lord of the Isles" and No. 999 were the most commanding objects of interest among all the exhibits in Transportation Building.

A WONDERFUL DECORATION IN GRAINS AND GRASSES.—Agricultural Hall was made, by the arts of the decorator, one of the most beautiful departments of the Great Fair. Those interested in products of the farm found more to please and gratify their tastes than exhibits of giant pumpkins, immense cereals and phenomenal growths that attested careful and intelligent cultivation. Nearly every State made displays of the products that showed the adaptation of their respective soils, and many of them combined the decorator's art in their displays of grains and grasses. Our photograph presents a view of a highly ornate section of the Great Hall, embellished with a marvelously tasteful and artistic arrangement of ears of corn, blades of grass, heads of wheat, etc. The columns were covered with exquisite designs, and the ceilings, friezes and cornices were frescoed with similar products, as shown in the charming illustration.

A VIEW OF THE SPANISH STATUARY SECTION.—Spain was less represented in the statuary exhibit of Art Hall than other leading nations, but the specimens shown were without exceptions noble examples of the work of the first sculptors of the age. In the picture above are to be seen a large plaster entitled, "A Struggle for Life," by Gines, taking for his subject a gladiator stricken mortally in the arena; another fine group is Parara's "Labor's Reward," also of plaster, and a sublime marble figure of "Christ and the Adulteress," by Rodolpho, elsewhere particularly described. "The Genius of War," is the work of Duque, represented as a man teasing an eagle. The architectural models shown are plaster designs for modern buildings, exhibited by Spanish architects.

INTERIOR OF THE FORESTRY BUILDING.—The department of Forestry at the World's Fair was one of the most complete and best managed of the many into which the great Exposition was divided. A large building was erected near the lake front in which the forest exhibit was made, an interior view of which is here presented. Comparatively few World's Fair visitors were attracted to the building, because of a belief, no doubt, that few things of interest were to be seen there; yet the exhibits there made were exceedingly attractive. Nearly every State, and many foreign nations, were represented in the displays, which included woods of the most beautiful grains, often polished like marble, and showing exquisite coloring, soft, varied, and reflective as glass. Many novelties were also exhibited, illustrative of the wide range of usefulness of wood for decorative purposes.

ROUTE OF THE INTRAMURAL RAILWAY.—A novelty and great convenience at the World's Fair was the elevated intramural railway, which pursued a somewhat tortuous course generally near the boundary of the grounds and at a height that afforded a most satisfactory view of nearly all the buildings. It was operated by electricity, the electric circuit being completed by the use of a third rail in preference to the trolley system. Our photograph pictures a section of the road that passed close to the State Buildings, the view being toward the south. Several of the Government and State structures are clearly shown in the picture, and likewise their several locations as respects each other. Upon the left-hand margin of the photograph is seen a small portion of the wall that protected the lake front of the grounds. The low-towered structure in the foreground is Iowa's Building.

MICHIGAN'S GRAIN DISPLAY.—Among the novel and picturesque exhibits that diversified the displays in Agricultural Building was that made by Michigan, as shown in the photograph above. In this beautiful exhibition wheat alone was seen, but it was fantastically arranged in the stalk and in the grain to represent many figures, the most interesting of which were the family of parents and children here shown, arrayed in the golden products of the field.

SOUTH DAKOTA'S EXHIBIT.—Scarcely less curious, and quite as interesting, was the structure built of flour sacks, constituting the milling exhibit of South Dakota. The display illustrated the growth of the flour-mill industry, from the wheezy old wind-mill to the colossal granite block typical of successful commerce. The exposition of flour from the wheat product of Dakota was a remarkable one, very helpful to the State as an evidence of the adaptation of her soil to the growth of the great cereals.

AGRICULTURAL PRODUCTS OF CALIFORNIA AND OKLAHOMA.—No one could easily tire of the magnificent and novel sights which changed like a kaleidoscope at every step of advance before the wondering gaze of visitors to Agricultural Building. In the views before us there is seen not a comparison but an associated picture of the grain exhibits of California and Oklahoma. The great stalks of corn displayed by the former were fourteen feet high and carried as many as three monster ears each, samples of which are seen disposed about the base of the shock, that is garnished with immense sheaves of wheat.

Oklahoma, though just emerged from the rule of Indian chiefs, made a grain exhibit which placed her in the front rank of great producing sections. The pavilion in which specimens of her grain was shown, was handsomely dressed in exquisite designs that presented a most beautiful sight, as well as illustrated the capacity of her soil, lately reclaimed from savages and disuse.

LAGOON AND TRANSPORTATION BUILDING.—In previous illustrations are presented the Golden Doorway of the Transportation Building, but in the present picture we have a charming three-quarters view of the front of that immense structure and the Lagoon upon which it bordered. The building was almost severely plain in its architectural treatment, but the decorator made a lavish display of his art in its exterior ornamentation. The great structure was particularly imposing as seen from the Lagoon, along which it extended its length of 960 feet, and its width was 256 feet. The cupola in the centre was 165 feet high and its galleries were reached by eight elevators. In addition to the building proper there was a triangular annex covering nine acres of ground, in which were numerous railroad tracks sixteen feet apart. Within the structure was a remarkable display of every conceivable thing appertaining to transportation, from a giant engine and luxurious coaches to a flying machine. It was a wonderful building with more wonderful exhibits.

THE SOUTHWEST TERRITORIES.—The photograph herewith gives an excellent view of the territorial building representing Arizona, Oklahoma and New Mexico. The architecture is Spanish, that fulfills conception of an airy yet languorous southern home, in the desert-begirted great Southwest. Specimens of giant cactus, bearded palm, beds of creeping cacti, and century plants, are living reminders of burning sands, but within the building were proofs of productive soil and lands rich in minerals. A broad veranda extended the length of the building, and a roof garden invited visitors to a charming retreat, shaded during the day by luxuriant vegetation and open enough by night to woo the soft winds and allow the moonbeams to struggle through, and cast their checkered rays upon the floor. It was an ideal resting place.

AN OLD DUTCH WINDMILL.—On the west bank of South Pond, back of the Agricultural Building, was a group of old-time windmills and the newest air motors. Among the former was a reproduction of an old Holland mill, which was built about the time of the close of the Revolution. The mill, though crotchety with infirmities, still swung its weather-beaten arms through the air and did duty as a cocoa grinder. Within its tower were Dutch maidens in bright dresses and wooden shoes serving cups of hot cocoa to visitors, and giving back glance for ogle, in the old-time style. The mill was a great curiosity, not only because it was a relic of the past, but also because the main timbers used in the tower were taken from a mill that ground flour and meal for the first settlers of Amsterdam, New York, and for soldiers of the Revolution.

SANTA BARBARA'S EXHIBIT OF OLIVE OIL.—Another one of the many curious and attractive displays in California's State Building was one which is shown in the photograph above. California has long been famous as a fruit-producing State as well as a big yielder of gold, but in the last few years her wealth has been immensely increased by the enlargement of her orchards of butternuts, almonds, and especially olives, the raising of these latter, and the extracting of olive oil, being now one of the State's most profitable industries. Santa Barbara County produces immense quantities of olives, and sustains numerous olive presses. The large obelisk, standing fifty feet high, shown in the illustration, was made of bottles of olive oil manufactured in the county. It was a novel exhibit and attracted very great attention.

UTAH TERRITORY BUILDING.—A very creditable structure was the one erected by Utah in which to receive visitors from the Territory, and in which to quarter the officers appointed to represent her at the Fair. The building, located in the extreme north portion of the grounds, was 50 x 90 feet, and of an ornate style of architecture, costing $18,500. The interior was handsomely finished and divided into many rooms, those in the second story being devoted to office quarters and Territorial exhibits. The approach was beneath an arch which was a counterpart of one in front of the official quarters of the president of the Mormon Church, Salt Lake City. To the right, and within the yard, was an excellent life-size statue of Brigham Young, the pedestal of which is seen in the illustration, between the columns of the eagle-supporting arch.

WEST FRONT OF THE GOVERNMENT BUILDING.—The view herewith is across Wooded Island looking directly at the west front of the Government Building. This structure commanded almost as much attention as any other building on the ground, notwithstanding it has been pronounced by architects as being twin brother to that other monstrosity, the Illinois Building. The domical treatment of these structures has been condemned, but it certainly made them prominent. This dome was 120 feet in diameter, and 275 feet high, to the pinnacle, while the building measured 350 x 420 feet, with projecting central bays on each front. The cost was $400,000. But if its architecture was more imposing than graceful, the marvelous range of exhibits which it contained compensated for all deficiencies of constructive style. Most of these remarkable displays are both illustrated and described in other pages of this serial.

THE BRAZILIAN GOVERNMENT BUILDING.—At the head of North Pond, in a sightly location, was the beautiful Brazilian structure here photographed. The ground plan was a Greek cross, with dimensions of 148 x 148 feet, and the style of architecture was the very ornate French Renaissance. In the façades and stylobate of the dome were Indian figures allegoric of the Brazilian Republic. The columns supporting the four pediments were of the chaste Corinthian style, with a rich entablature. The appearance was charming, and the design was both appropriate and convenient. Cost of the building was $90,000.

THE OLD LOG CABIN.—Close to the Model Workingman's Home and the French Colonies exhibit was the Old Log Cabin, a typical home of the pioneer, erected by some Louisville distillers in which to make their exhibits. The materials used in its construction were logs, tile, and stucco, while the quaint building was enclosed by a rustic fence and surrounded by a charming flower-garden. Among the exhibits were samples of whiskey, and an old time still, common enough a hundred years ago, but which survives now only in secluded sections where the moonshiner is not liable to the

THREE DANCING GIRLS FROM EGYPT.—Visitors to the Midway Plaisance theatres will recognize at once in the photographs herewith three girls who delighted spectators by their contortion dances in the Egyptian theatre. While their exhibitions were sensationally, if not sensually, amusing, the girls were not otherwise calculated to attract attention save it be by their immodest costumes. Writers of Oriental stories have created the impression among the uninformed that houris of the East are sylph-like and beautiful; but close contact reveals them as we behold them here, destitute of animation, formless as badly-stuffed animals, as homely as owls, and graceless as stall-fed bovines. But truth compels us to add that the dancing girls in the Midway were not the best types of their race either in form or character, and that their abdominal muscles were the only portions of anatomy or mind which showed any cultivation, while these, to their shame, were displayed to serve the basest uses.

A COMPANY OF SOUDANESE.—From the intertropical regions of Africa came the troupe of Soudanese photographed above. The space along the Midway was so fully occupied before their arrival at Chicago that it was necessary to locate them in the rear of the Cairo street, so hidden from the throng of visitors that a great many persons failed to observe them. These people from equatorial lands of the savage continent were rather small of stature and wore a fierce and repulsive aspect. They were intensely black, but yet had few of the physiognomic features of the negro, aside from color, and are brave to a degree as well as intensely zealous, characteristics well proved by the heroism displayed by them as followers of the Mahdi. They were quick in action, inclined to be humorous, and very proud of the trophies of human bones which some of them wore. The women were better featured than the men, and the little children were as comical as young monkeys, affording infinite amusement to visitors. The men were armed with swords and lances, with which they gave spirited exhibits, at times simulating a mad encounter.

THE IRISH VILLAGE AND BLARNEY CASTLE.—To the efforts of Mrs. Ernest Hart and Lady Aberdeen were due the reproduction of Blarney Castle and the construction of the Irish Village shown in the photograph. The location of these remarkable exhibits was on the south side of the Midway, near the Illinois Central Railroad Station. Facing the gate of the Village, which was towered and crenelated in faithful replication of the St. Lawrence Gate at Drogheda, were ruins of the great banqueting hall of Donegal Castle, and all around were signs of village industry, busy girls weaving, embroidering, spinning, crocheting and other semi-domestic and manufacturing employments. The Village occupied several acres of space, and among the many curiosities there exhibited were ecclesiastical vestments, wood carvings, jewelry, paintings, a round tower 120 feet high, hole stones, cromlechs, crosses, iron work, and, most interesting of all, the Wishing Chair of the Giants' Causeway. Within the enclosure also was a reproduction of Blarney Castle, with what was averred to be the genuine Blarney stone hanging right where so many thousands have kissed it, and then gone away to be disappointed.

A GROUP OF ESQUIMAUX.—Near the entrance gate at Fifty-seventh street was the Esquimau village, comprising a population of fifty-seven natives, of all ages, and six dogs. It was an interesting, even though a rather repulsive, place to visit, replete with curiosities peculiar to these Arctic people. In the village were displayed sledges, spears, canoes, stone lamps, images, ivory carvings, seal oil, and whales' blubber. The natives occasionally wore their fur clothing in the early days of the Fair, but during the summer months they suffered greatly from the heat.

THE HAYTIAN EXHIBIT.—Within the Hayti Building, elsewhere described, were natural products, and displays of the deft handiwork of those West Indies people, including coffee, sugar, liqueurs, syrups, minerals, plants, and native women's work in the form of such articles as hats, matting, chairs, rugs, etc. Here were to be seen a great variety of useful manufactures wrought from palm fibres, and a hut constructed of the same material, illustrating the extensive use made by the natives of the palm tree.

BUILDINGS THAT REPRESENTED THE FRENCH COLONIES.—A portion of the French Government Exhibit were buildings typical of the French possessions in various parts of the world, making specially prominent the Island Colonies, as shown in the illustration, but including also possessions in Central Africa and Tonquin. Some of the structures were light booths made of bamboo, bark and leaves, but others were substantial and a few ornate, after the manner of the architecture of the countries which they typified.

A SPICE EXHIBIT.—The second illustration shows an exhibit made in Manufactures Building by the firm whose name is prominently displayed. The arrangement of the goods in cases was very unique, and the pavilion was rendered grotesque by a Chinese design ornamented with heads of indescribable creatures that seemed to laugh, leer, scowl and threaten the passing crowds.

INTERIOR OF THE ANTHROPOLOGICAL BUILDING.—On the main floor of the building, as will be seen by the view here printed, were exhibited collections illustrative of North American tribes, comprising costumes, utensils, implements, ornaments, etc. In the same section were exhibited specimens of the handiwork of British Columbian Indians and original peoples of Canada. As a central group in the main hall was the very instructive exhibit made by Greece, showing ancient Grecian art and archæology chronologically arranged, on both sides of which were arranged small exhibits from Assyria, Egypt and Rome. Extending across the hall was a section devoted to religious symbols and folk-lore, where were displayed idols, ceremonial objects, amulets, charms and various other articles connected with religious observances of all times and countries. The collection was the most complete that was ever made, and formed an exhibition of extraordinary interest.

A SIDE VIEW OF THE AUSTRIAN SECTION.—Our photograph represents a side entrance to the Austrian Section, in Manufactures Building, shortly before the Exposition was officially opened. There were numerous visitors to the grounds for months before the sections were even ready to receive the displays, and our picture herewith was taken while workmen were putting the Austrian house in order for the wonderful exhibits which were brought into it two weeks later, and elsewhere shown and described in this series.

JAPANESE EXHIBIT IN ART HALL.—The far-away country of Japan, the land of imaginary demons and dragons, but withal a country whose civilization is both ancient and great, was becomingly represented at the Great Fair, and particularly in the splendid Art Palace. Our picture presents a view of a part of the Japanese section, in which the Government colors are conspicuous. The very large bronze eagle in the foreground was the work of Okazaki, who has never seen America. Other figures are a wood carving representing "Shoko, the Devil Driver," by Takenouchi, and "KinKaji, a Temple," the work of Hada. In the room were also several very handsome paintings, screens, and beautifully carved ivory figures, evidencing the refined tastes, splendid conceptions, and remarkable artistic creations of the Japanese.

EGYPTIAN GIRL IN STREET OF CAIRO.—In all countries where Moslemism prevails it is common for ladies to wear a veil over the lower half of the face when appearing on the street. The custom is not so rigidly observed as formerly, and in India it has almost entirely disappeared. Among the Persians and Egyptians, however, it is still a general practice, and will no doubt continue, for in those countries the immigration of foreigners has failed to influence the customs of the natives. In the street of Cairo at the World's Fair there was exhibited the peculiar manners of the Egyptians, and a veiled lady was of course one of the curious objects displayed, though she did not always appear in that unsightly disguise, thus proving that she was not a slave to this requirement of all Mohammedan women.

A SECTION OF NORTH POND.—The photograph here presented shows a large portion of the lagoon known as North Pond, and some of the important buildings bordering thereon. The columnated structure on the right hand is the Palace of Fine Arts, showing the electric launch landing at the south front, and across the lagoon, slightly southeast, is Illinois Building, and in the west are to be caught glimpses of several State buildings. On the left shore, adjoining Illinois' State structure, may be indistinctly discerned several white ducks, whose presence in the north grounds was tolerated through some inscrutable judgment that certainly had no remote relation to wisdom. Visitors to this section were offended by the noisome odors and indescribable filth that distinguished the south shore, produced by scores of these fowls, which marred the beauty of that portion of the grounds, and actually brought it into disrepute.

A SCENE OF MARVELOUS SPLENDOR.—The vista here presented is one of almost inconceivable magnificence, exposing as it does the jewel-setting in the ring of World's Fair architectural splendors. There is about this view a realization of the imaginary cities built by genii to amaze the califs of Oriental fancy; a dream of fairyland perpetuated in an actual creation; a marvelous vision developed into substance. The photograph exhibits the scene with a vividness and clearness that seems to bring us into the real presence of the glories that spread themselves in a panorama of bewildering beauty before the wonderful Court of Honor. Playing fountains in iridescent hues, sculptured columns, graceful statuary simulating nature, a lake whose bosom is flecked with pretty crafts, bridges of handsome proportions, and buildings as grand and charming as Phidias ever conceived, more splendid than kings of Greece or Carthage ever saw. The view is from the corner of Machinery Hall looking north-eastward to Manufactures Building.

THE CEYLON COURT.—One of the most curiously ornate buildings erected by foreign nations was that known as the Ceylon Court, a structure having two wings facing respectively north and south, projecting from an octagonal rotunda. The extreme length was 145 feet and the width 50 feet. The style of architecture was Dravidian, adopted from the ancient temples whose ruins are so frequently to be met with in Ceylon. It was constructed entirely of native woods, that were fashioned and made ready for joining together before being shipped to America. It contained four beautifully carved stairways, which were also copied from ancient temples, with figures of evil spirits, cobras, geese, and fabulous creatures. The decorations were marvelously rich and intricate, and the cost was $60,000.

THE WASHINGTON STATE BUILDING.—In remarkable contrast with the above, was Washington's State Building, a very large structure 140 x 220 feet, built of immense logs as an exhibit of her lumber resources. Some of these were 52 inches in diameter and 120 feet long, the largest that the railroad was able to transport. The building was one of the great features of the Fair, as was also the varied display of native products

GLADSTONE'S AX AND WOOD EXHIBIT.—All the civilized world has heard of Gladstone as a wood-chopper, whose sturdy arm has shown itself in Hawarden forest as well as in Parliament. It was proper therefore to place on exhibition, in the Forestry Building, an ax which the great Prime Minister and statesman used, accompanied by written documents proving its distinguished ownership. But probably more interesting than the ax were the sections of trees shown, one of which was from the greatest of California redwoods, the girth of which at the time of the landing of Columbus is indicated by the arrow. The bamboos partially shown in the picture extended to a height of seventy-five feet.

REPRODUCTION OF RUINS OF YUCATAN.—Elsewhere is shown a larger but less distinct view of a reproduction, in papier-maché, of the ruins of ancient Uxmal, or House of the Nuns, in Yucatan. This archæologic architectural exhibit was located near the Alaska village, with which it was in curious contrast, thus bringing together in rivalry strange specimens from tropical and arctic climes. One, however, showed a high state of extinct civilization, the other presenting examples of present savagery.

BUFFALO BILL'S WILD WEST SHOW.—The World's Fair did not wholly monopolize the interest of visitors, for there were many side-shows near by which secured a liberal patronage. Next to the Fair itself, however, was Buffalo Bill's Wild West Exhibition, which occupied ten acres of space between Sixty-first and Sixty-third streets, just outside the Exposition grounds, and entertained in a period of six months 4,000,000 of people. His troupe comprised two hundred Indians, of various tribes, and companies each of American, English, French, German, Mexican, Cossack and Arabian cavalry, besides cowboys, vaqueros, female riders, dancing dervishes, athletes, rifle experts, bucking ponies, a herd of buffaloes, and other attractions expositional of the great plains and rough riders of the world. In the photograph above, Colonel Cody (Buffalo Bill) is seen standing at his tent door, with Manager Frank Burke on his left, behind a bevy of fearless female riders.

A PANORAMIC VIEW FROM THE NORTHEAST.—A very charming sight is presented in the above photograph, taking in a very large section of the Fair grounds and picturing with great distinctness the Merchants' Tailoring Building, in the foreground, and the massive Woman's Building. The former was 94 feet square, of a Grecian temple style, and as handsomely finished in the interior as its beautiful exterior appearance might indicate. The walls were splendidly frescoed with eight scenes, representing as many periods in dress evolution and reform, and the details were more elaborate than are to be seen in any permanent structure of the present time. The steps leading into the water, beautiful bridges on either side, and embowered with trees, the building was a model of picturesqueness and magnificent repose, a suggestion of the Phidian age of architectural splendor.

THE AUSTRIAN SECTION IN MANUFACTURES BUILDING.—The beautiful view that is here presented was taken from the gallery of Manufactures Building, presenting at one glance the avenues and arrangement of one of the most remarkable displays made at the Exposition. The magnificent portal, fronting on Columbia avenue, which the centre aisle of the building was called, is shown in the photograph, through which visitors passed to the display, though the exhibits were also reached by side aisles. The particular display in this section was of Glassware, and Hungarian and Bohemian goods of exquisite patterns and the most charming coloring.

A WONDERFUL VISION SOUTHWARD FROM THE ROOF OF MANUFACTURES BUILDING.—The most charming panorama that ever startled the eye of a beholder is photographed in much of its naturalness above. The view is from the roof promenade of Manufactures Building looking southward. What a picturesque and magnificent stretch of gleaming buildings and opalescent lake! The palace-like structure immediately in front, across the Grand Basin, is Agricultural Hall, with a beautiful plaza that emphasized its royal splendor and magnificent sculptuary that crowned it with glory. On the right there rises in the distance two tall white shafts, one of which we recognize as a rostral column and the other an obelisk. On the left the beauties are multiplied, for we observe the golden heroic figure of the Republic, and behind the statue are architectural wonders which we know to be the Peristyle and Casino, while below these are seen the Convent of La Rabida, the Krupp, and Shoe and Leather Buildings, then fades the glimmering landscape into the steel-blue of lake and distance.

A MODEL SCHOOL FOR THE EDUCATION OF HEAD AND HANDS.—The Children's Building, between Horticultural Hall and the Woman's Building, was a revelation to many persons who visited the Fair, especially the exhibits and provisions for youthful care and training which it contained. The gymnasium, and crèche, or nursery, were models of completeness and examples of the wisdom displayed by the Women Managers at the Fair. But there were other displays in the Educational Building, a room of which is shown in the accompanying photograph. Here was exhibited a combination method by which children are educated not only in the common school branches, but also in the manual arts, a polytechnic institute, in which girls and boys alike are instructed in the arts, sciences and mechanics. It was a rather odd sight to see small girls bending over a carpenter's bench; but while the trade is not suitable for the female sex, a knowledge of construction and the use of tools has been considered valuable both as a recreation and for practical purposes.

INTERIOR OF THE EAST SIDE OF MANUFACTURES BUILDING.—A very expansive view is here presented, representing the displays made in the east side of Manufactures Building. The picture gives an excellent idea of the arrangement and appearance of the displays in that mammoth structure, where products from every part of the earth were exhibited, nation vying with nation as firm were contested with firm, for the honor that pronouncement of superior merit would give. Millions of dollars' worth of property, in divers forms and of nearly every conceivable kind known to the commercial world, was here displayed in Expositional rivalry, and there were crowns without scars, attesting the truth of the declaration, "Peace hath her victories no less renowned than war."

A LEMONADE VENDOR WITH EGYPTIAN JUG.—The photograph here presented exhibits a curiosity which attracted no small share of the attention bestowed upon foreigners in the Midway Plaisance. The person here shown was a peripatetic, in that he wandered about over nearly every part of the Fair grounds, selling a tasteless lemonade, at five cents per cup. Curiosity prompted many to buy merely to see how he drew the pale water from his strange vessel, and they were thus compensated, for expecting to be surprised they were not disappointed. Instead of displaying something very novel, however, as seemed to be indicated by the structure of the vessel and the ornate attachments on its neck, the lemonade peddler surprised his patrons by merely twisting the large turned piece on the end, which was in fact the simplest kind of a faucet, and tilting his skin bottle the water flowed freely out, into the decorated cup which he holds in his right hand. "Is that all?" was a remark made by many of his astonished customers, and they never patronized him more than once.

DONKEY BOYS IN THE CAIRO STREET.—Joseph and his donkey will be instantly recognized in the accompanying photograph by those who visited the street of Cairo. The larger fellow on the right was usually seen at the rear end of a camel belaboring his animal with a stout stick, or soliciting persons to take a flyer on the ship of the desert as it lay becalmed upon its carpet. The picture shows the kind of saddle which Egyptians use, a hummock rising in front of the rider in imitation of a big ham, or an Oriental water-bottle, but not less comfortable than saddles with which we are accustomed. The trappings, however, are very suggestive of short-stop animals, whereas in fact donkeys are partial to long stops. No one ever saw an Egyptian donkey move fast enough to unseat a rider by stopping short, hence the saddle and breeching are rather designed to deceive than to serve any useful purpose.

A CARNIVAL IN THE STREET OF CAIRO.—There was something interesting being enacted in the Cairo street almost constantly, to which is due the immense patronage which that attraction received. People would go once to see the donkey drivers, the veiled women and the bazaars, but it required other exhibitions to draw them a second time, and these were provided by a series of entertainments, such as a wedding procession, a sleight-of-hand performance, a procession of veiled women, a musical concert of kettle-drum and pipe, a carnival, etc. The photograph herewith represents a semi-masque carnival, in which the attractions are a man in the guise of a bear being led by the master of ceremonies, three veiled women, dragomans, camel riders, priests and donkey boys. The procession was distinctively Egyptian, and afforded great amusement to visitors, as much by the comicalities of the participants as by their strange costumes.

AN ALGERIAN GIRL.—The Algerian and Tunisian village on the Plaisance was an exceedingly interesting section of the side-show to the Fair. It comprised a reproduction of a street in Algiers, desert tent, Moorish café, Kabyle house, a street of Tunis, and a theatre with a seating capacity of 1000 people. Connected with the latter were fifty performers, musicians, jugglers and dancing girls, one of the latter being shown in the above photograph. Her dress, it will be observed, is elaborately bedizened with gewgaws which North Africans and Orientals lavishly affect, but there is an absence of the style and abbreviation of costume which dancing girls in other theatres of the Midway adopted to draw patronage at the sacrifice of modesty. The Moorish girls accompanied their dancing with the soft tinkling of wristlet and necklace bells, and their movements were more graceful than were those of the Egyptian and Persian dancers, but there was a resemblance in the muscular exercise, which constituted a chief attraction of the exhibition, though less flagrant, because the Algerian girls were more decently clothed.

SWORDSMEN FROM DAMASCUS.—Some very skillful swordsmen and lance throwers came out of the East to exhibit their dexterity before World's Fair visitors. The two men photographed above were natives of Syria, residents of Damascus, the old city of Biblical fame, the commercial eye of the East twenty centuries ago, the city made famous also by the Damascus blades manufactured there for the soldiery of Saladdin, and Solomon the Magnificent, foes of the chivalrous crusaders. The exhibitions given by these two Syrians were very exciting, as they fought savagely, but always so adroitly that neither one was able to harm the other.

A GROUP OF ARABS AND TURKS.—The photograph herewith is of two parties, Turks and Arabs, presented together to show the contrast between these two closely associated peoples. The three on the left, it is proper to state, are Europeanized Turks, who have rubbed up against civilization until they show much of its polish. There is so little in common between them and their brethren of Asiatic Turkey that they would scorn association with the latter. These three Turks came to Chicago as managers of Midway Plaisance theatres. The three men on the right are from Arabian cities, one of them being a resident of Mecca, and having seen considerable of the world, and improved their advantages, they are of a much higher order of intelligence than are the Arab street fakirs who are frequently seen in this country. The Arab child in the centre of the group was eight years of age and uncommonly bright. In his hands he holds a shield made of hippopotamus hide, used as a guard in contests between Arabian swordsmen, described in another portfolio of this series.

LIGHTHOUSE AND LIFE-SAVING STATION.—On the plaza, in front of the Government Building, was the neat and pretty camp of the life-saving corps, and a model of a government lighthouse. All the paraphernalia employed in the saving of life when shipwreck occurs within sight of shore, was displayed, and the company of life-guards were put through a drill nearly every day for the benefit alike of practice and the edification of visitors.

THE VIKING SHIP.—Our photograph represents the strange craft known as the Viking Ship as she appeared under full sail. This remarkable vessel is a copy of a ship discovered in a burial mound at Gokstad, Norway, 1880, where it had been buried probably in the tenth century, being the kind of oar and sail boat in which the Vikings or sea-rovers of the North crossed the ocean, discovered Iceland, Greenland, and thence reached the shores of America in the year 985. The Viking Ship was only fifty feet long and was an open boat, but she safely crossed the Atlantic under the command of Magnus Anderson and sailed through the lakes to Chicago.

THE MAMMOTH FERRIS WHEEL.—Greatest of all the many wonders exhibited at the Columbian Exposition was the monster spider-web cycle known as the Ferris Wheel, located in the Midway Plaisance. This remarkable product of inventive genius was designed and constructed under the direction of G. W. Ferris, superintendent of one of the large bridge companies of America. The forgings were made at Detroit; the axle, 33 inches in diameter, 45 feet long and weighing 56 tons, was the largest single piece of steel ever cast in this country. This colossal shaft rested upon steel towers 137 feet high, and the lifting of it into place required the use of a derrick bigger, taller and stronger than was ever made before. The wheel was 264 feet in diameter, between the rims of which, separated by a distance of 28½ feet, 36 cars were suspended, each having a capacity of 60 passengers. It was perfectly balanced, and was turned by a sprocket-chain, attached to an engine of 2000 horse-power, with an engine of like power held in reserve. The time occupied in making one revolution was about twenty minutes, and the price of passage, for two revolutions, was fifty cents. Cost of the wheel was $362,000, but the earnings paid the cost in three months after it was put in motion, and the profits of its operation were much greater in the latter months of the Fair.

AN ODALISQUE FROM THE SERAGLIO.—Among the several dancers and female performers in the Midway theatres, there were less than half a dozen that supported their claims to beauty with even passably good looks, or graceful figures. The most pleasing was undoubtedly the little Javanese actress, described elsewhere, and next to her in the eyes of admirers was the Moorish girl, whose picture is here shown. She was heralded by the Algerian Concessionaire as an Odalisque, fresh from the Seraglio, and the Sultan's favorite. This was rhetorical, even if not true, so she was accepted as a beauty and invested with a mystery that made her a very interesting personage. She danced in the Algerian theatre, and was for a while exceedingly popular, but she was less fascinating to young men visitors to the Fair than Fatima, of the Persian theatre, who, while not so pretty, was more lithesome, and executed the *danse du ventre* with a wild abandon that called for repression by the authorities.

FROM THE LAKE FRONT TO THE PLAISANCE.—In the upper left-hand corner of the group of pictures on this page is a photograph of the United States Model Army Hospital, which was located immediately north of Manufactures Building, in which was exhibited by the War Department an army hospital ready for operations. On the right at the top of the group is a photograph of a life-boat mounted for launching. The life service corps were located on the plaza near the Government Building, and were put through daily drills with their boats, near the battle-ship *Illinois*. In the lower left-hand corner is a picture of the building on the Plaisance in which were exhibited forty ladies of as many nationalities, dressed in the costumes peculiar to their respective countries. It was called a "Congress of Beauty," but the term was misleading because, sad to confess, there was very much less of beauty than was claimed. On the right is a picture of an Arab and his performing goat, though in the photograph his only audience is a much interested monkey

A QUARTET OF STATE BUILDINGS.—The first picture at the top, to the left, represents Missouri's Building at the Fair; that at the right, the Kansas Building; at the bottom toward the left, Minnesota; and to the right, Wisconsin. Missouri's Building was of a composite style, with large central dome, flanked by Moorish towers, and many ornate features. It was built by Missouri mechanics, and, as far as practicable, of material produced in the State. The cost was $40,000. The Kansas Building was cruciform in plan, 135 x 140 feet, and of a warm, picturesque style, with bas-reliefs in front of the tower, designed to represent the State at the time of her admission into the Union, armed for struggle, and also as she appears to-day, abounding in wealth and resources. Cost, $35,000. Minnesota's Building occupied a ground space of 80 x 90 feet, and was 41 feet high to the main cornice, the style of architecture being Italian Renaissance. On the front portico were statues of Hiawatha and Minnehaha, contributed by the school children of the State and the Woman's Auxiliary Board, under which were lines from Longfellow. Cost, $40,000. Wisconsin's Building had a frontage of 90 feet, with a depth of 50 feet, exclusive of its porches. The first story was of brown stone and pressed brick, the second of dimension shingles, the combination producing a very pretty effect. In front were also columns of polished granite, giving the building a substantial appearance, suggestive of a rich club house, which was increased by the contrasting colors in which it was painted. Cost, $30,000.

SCENES IN THE MIDWAY PLAISANCE.—In the views here given are represented the Temple of Luxor and two Egyptian obelisks, which were to be seen at the western end of the street of Cairo, very excellent reproductions of the historic representation of Luxor's wondrous temple on the Nile, and the obelisks which stand as a mark of the ancient civilization of Egypt. The second picture at the top of the page is the Persian Palace, in which disciples of Zoroaster displayed rugs, scimeters, damasks, curios, and a great variety of Oriental wares. The third picture is an oblique rear view of the Texas Building, elsewhere described. The lower left-hand photograph shows the Algerian Theatre, which had a seating capacity of 1100 people, and in which dramas were enacted to pleased multitudes, who had to rely upon an interpreter for a knowledge of what the actors said and did. The photograph to the right presents an excellent view of the building in which the Libbey Glass Company, of Toledo, Ohio, made their manufacturing exhibit. Here were shown the many interesting processes of making glassware, from the mixing, blowing, and forming to the cutting and decorating. In one department there was also displayed the strange work of spinning and weaving of glass into dresses, neckties, handkerchiefs, napkins, bonnets, lamp-shades, etc. The building, which contained also furnaces and a bazaar, was large enough to accommodate 5000 visitors at one time.

A PLEASANT VARIATION OF SCENES.—The first picture here shown represents the old whaling bark, "Progress," an exhibit from New Bedford, Mass., that lay in South Pond near the Ethnographic exhibit. She was built in 1841 and has passed through many vicissitudes of storm and whale-hunting. In her saloon were displayed all the weapons and paraphernalia used in whaling and also mementoes of a disaster that occurred in 1871, when thirty-three whaling vessels were caught in the ice and their crews rescued by the "Progress." On the right, at the top, is a photograph of the whaleback vessel, "Christopher Columbus," that carried passengers between the pier at the foot of Van Buren street, Chicago, and the Exposition grounds. The third photograph shows an electric launch landing opposite the Fisheries Building, and the fourth picture exhibits the north loop of the Intra-Mural elevated electric railroad.

FOUR OF THE FAR WESTERN STATES.—The photographs above represent the State buildings of Montana, on the left, at the top of the group; Nebraska on the right; North Dakota at the left, and South Dakota on the right, at the bottom of the group. Montana's Building was a one-story structure, 62 feet front by 113 feet deep, constructed of wood and iron, and covered with staff and glass. Above the arched entrance was a miniature mountain peak, on which stood the statue of an elk nine feet high. Cost of the building $15,000. Nebraska was represented very handsomely by a structure of Colonial style of architecture, which covered an area of 60 x 100 feet. On each side was a portico with four massive columns extending the full height of the second story, supporting a plain gable. The walls were made of staff, colored to represent stone, so that the appearance, while severely plain, was that of a most substantial and expensive building. The cost, however, was only $15,000. North Dakota also had a Colonial style building, of a hospitable type, the front elevation being rendered attractive by porches, with columns reaching the full height of the second story, the roof of which was a balustrade. Dimensions of the building were 40 x 70 feet, and the cost $11,000. The sister State, South Dakota, was represented by a building 60 x 100 feet, with two stories each fourteen feet in height. The exterior was coated with cement, finished in imitation of stone, which gave the structure an elegant as well as grand appearance. The treatment of the front elevation was similar—save that it was semi-circular in shape—to that which distinguished her northern sister. Cost $12,000.

AMONG THE STATE BUILDINGS.—The four States represented by the buildings above pictured were Massachusetts at the top, to the left; Ohio at the right, New Jersey at the bottom, to the left; and Kentucky on the right. Massachusetts' Building was an imitation of John Hancock's residence, which stood in Colonial times on Beacon Hill, Boston, near the State Capitol. It was a palatial, though old style, mansion, 120 x 65 feet, with double parlors, which, when thrown together, formed a room 80 x 25 feet. The floor was of marble, the walls covered with tiles, mantels in imitation of the Dutch houses of old Amsterdam, and the beams and rafters exposed after the Norwegian style. Cost $50,000. Ohio's Building was a social headquarters, and contained no exhibits. Its dimensions were 100 x 80 feet, and the style Italian Renaissance, with bay-windows, porticos, terraces and other pretty and inviting features. In front was a semi-circular portico with eight Ionic columns, supporting an open balustrade, and the roof was covered with red tile. Cost of the building about $50,000. New Jersey's Building, like that of Massachusetts, was of Colonial type, in imitation of Washington's headquarters at Morristown during the winter of 1779–80. There was no attempt at ornamentation, and the building was used wholly by the State Commissioners, and as a meeting place for visitors from the State. Cost $20,000. Kentucky's Building was 75 x 95 feet, and represented the Southern Colonial style of homestead, that seems to invite to generous hospitality. The main entrance and Corinthian columns gave it the appearance of a court house, which, however, was relieved by a semi-circular porch on the side, in front of which was a statue of Daniel Boone. Cost $30,000.

A PAGE OF VARIETIES.—The two buildings shown at the top of the page are the State structures of Maine and Texas, and at the bottom is a photograph of the company of Samoans brought to the Fair, and of the north front of the Fine Art Palace, both of which latter are described elsewhere in this serial. The Maine Building occupied a triangular lot in the New England group of buildings, for which reason it was made octagon in shape, sixty-five feet in diameter, and two stories high, with a high dome surmounted by a lantern, the floor of which was sixty-four feet above the ground, and the pinnacle eighty-five feet. The first story was constructed of granite from Maine quarries, and the varieties used exhibited many different hues and various texture, the effects being rendered more variable by reason of some of the blocks being rough, while the exterior of others was carved and polished. The second story contained four balconies projecting over the granite walls, and were roofed with slate from the Monson quarries. Cost of the building $20,000. The Texas Building was built with funds raised through the efforts of ladies of that State, and was of a character that reflected great credit not only upon Texan ladies, but upon the State itself. A feature of the building was its assembly rooms, fifty-six feet square and twenty feet high, provided with ceilings of art glass, in the centre of which was a mosaic Texas steer. The style of architecture was Spanish, and the garden which surrounded it was a graceful blending of shrubbery, fruits and flowers, that are native alike to Mexico and Texas. The building was towered, after the Spanish style, and the wide corner porches were distinctively Southern, affording opportunity for ornate treatment, which was not neglected. Cost $40,000.

A GROUP OF STATE BUILDINGS.—In the photographs herewith are the State structures of Virginia, at the upper left-hand corner; Indiana on the right; Vermont at the lower left-hand corner, and West Virginia at the right. Virginia's Building was a reproduction of Washington's Mount Vernon residence, which is the shrine of so many patriots. The structure was 94 x 32 feet, and had two stories and an attic, with large columns in front extending from the porch to the roof cornice. There were twenty-five rooms in the building, as there are in the original, one of which was Washington's chamber and in which he died; also the room in which Mrs. Washington expired, was shown, reproduced with striking fidelity. Cost of the structure $15,000. Indiana was represented by a Gothic structure 53 x 152 feet, much of the space being occupied by wide verandas of a most imposing and picturesque character. The building was three stories in height, the first of native gray sandstone, and the others of wood and staff. A very pleasing effect was produced by the composite architecture exhibiting towers, turrets and cathedral windows, with tall spires rising to a height of 150 feet. Cost $45,000. Rhode Island's Building was a parallelogram 39 x 34 feet, flanked by a north and south porch the full width of the structure. Being severely Greek, the rear entrance was between fluted Ionic pilasters, and the front was three semi-circular arched openings with columns surmounted by Ionic entablature and decorated moldings of beautiful patterns. Cost $20,000. West Virginia's Building was of Colonial style, with broad piazzas almost encircling the structure. Space covered was 58 x 123 feet, and all the material used was from the State. The exterior was plain, but the furnishings were rich and the displays shown in the building were of great value. Cost $20,000.

AN INDIAN TEA ROOM.—One of the most sumptuously elegant rooms of the many handsomely furnished cosies and apartments at the World's Fair was the India Tea Room shown in the photograph herewith. The furnishings were richest damasks, beautifully carved chairs, and exquisitely inlaid tables. The service, too, was no less elegant, being the most delicate wares manufactured in the Orient. The photograph represents an India priest and a rajah, the latter laving his hands, from a bowl held by the priest, after the custom of Moslems and Bhuddists alike, before taking refreshment of tea. This room was connected with the India display in Manufactures Building, but being private, in a measure, comparatively few Fair visitors enjoyed the privilege of its inspection.

THE ELECTRIC FOUNTAIN PLAYING.—At the two eastern corners of the Court of Honor, flanking the Columbian Barge, were beautiful fountains, the northeastern one being shown in the photograph. They were called Electric Fountains, because in the basins were arranged electric globes of various colors, and so carefully hidden that their presence was hardly suspected. When the water was playing at night and the lights turned on, a scene of bewitching splendor was produced that has rarely been equaled by the ingenious arts of the electrician. The fountain was composed of a large number of jets, through which the water shot up at different heights and in a variety of forms, as exhibited in the illustration, rendering it even in the day-time an object of extravagant beauty.

A PERFORMANCE IN THE EGYPTIAN THEATRE.—An excellent photographic view is here afforded of a dancing performance in the Egyptian Theatre, an attraction which usually entertained fair-sized audiences continuously from 10 a. m. until 10 p. m. The picture shows one of the dancing girls executing a movement which was more shuffle and muscular contortion than dance, accompanying her exercises with castanets in each hand. The dance du ventre, as the movement is known, and which was executed by girls not only in the Egyptian Theatre, but also in the Persian, Turkish, and, with some modification, in the Moorish Theatres, on the Plaisance, is a suggestively lascivious contorting of the abdominal muscles, which is extremely ungraceful and almost shockingly disgusting. Curiosity prompted many to view the performance, but very few remained more than five minutes before this was fully satisfied. Only one girl danced at a time, but others were in reserve, so that as one retired another promptly succeeded her, thus making the performance continuous throughout the day and evening.

ALLEGORIC STATUARY.—The Administration and Agricultural Buildings were decorated with many pieces of strikingly expressive allegoric statuary, some of which are presented in other numbers of "The Magic City" series, and two of which strong examples are photographed above. The group at the top represents a mother firing her son with ambition and patriotism, and the unfinished group below presents in allegory Father Sage teaching a child wisdom and truth. The size of these figures may be estimated by the comparison afforded by the photograph of a workman who is seen standing between the sage and child. All of the large plaster statuary that occupied vantage places about the Fair grounds, and which decorated the buildings, were formed upon the immediate premises under the direction of the greatest sculptors of the age, and though they were made to endure for a short time, such great attention was paid to detail and effect that had they been similarly fashioned in marble they would still have ranked very high as splendid specimens of the sculptor's art.

A VIEW OF THE CAIRO STREET.—No other exhibition or reproduction in the Midway Plaisance was so interesting and entertaining as the Street of Cairo. Passing through a gate, before which stood a camel supporting an Egyptian who incessantly beat two kettledrums, the visitor came at once into the presence of distinctively Egyptian surroundings. The street was a faithful reproduction of a principal thoroughfare of Cairo known as Bein el Kasrein, lined with booths, mosques and singularly quaint but ornate buildings, such as are excellently shown in the above photograph. The street was about two hundred yards long, with curiosities crowded into every foot of the way, and at the western end was a theatre in which Egyptian girls gave their dancing performances. A little to the left was the museum, in which wax imitations of the mummies of ancient rulers of Egypt were shown, and beyond this was the tomb of Apis—the sacred bull. The latticed windows, pretty balconies, graceful verandas and inviting courts were architectural features that added very much to the attractions of the street.

SOUDANESE GIRLS.—The photograph herewith exhibits three Soudanese girls, who belonged to the company that was brought to the Fair and exhibited in a rather circumscribed enclosure near the Cairo street. These people were rather short of stature and of an ebony black; but while members of the Negroid race, they were distinguished by typical characteristics at decided variance with the negro. The facial features were more classic and animated, and the hair, while curly, was long and easily trained. Usually, the women wore the hair in corkscrew curls, and to a length that touched the shoulders, and their costume was Egyptian, save that they were more fond of gewgaws. The girls shown above ranged in age from sixteen to twenty years; they were vivacious and far from prudish, but it would be a very imaginary person who could discover signs of beauty in their faces or grace in their movements.

THE NEW YORK STATE BUILDING.—The Great Empire State was most fittingly and splendidly represented at the World's Fair by the building shown in the photograph above. Its location was near the Art Gallery, between the State buildings of Pennsylvania and Massachusetts. The design was of a palatial order, slightly Moresque, and of an original type, magnificently embellished with terraces, porticos, verandas and balconies, suggestive of a tropical mansion where artistic taste had joined hands with great wealth to produce a structure of the most beautiful character. In size the building was 142 x 214 feet, with two towers rising to a height of 96 feet. Charmingly decorative as was the exterior, the finishing and furnishing of the interior was of a much more sumptuous character, in resemblance of a palace wherein Solomon himself might have dwelt with pride. The approach to the entrance was by a broad flight of steps ushering the visitor into an immense hall lavishly furnished and splendidly decorated with great pieces of statuary and other splendid objects of art. A grand staircase led by easy ascent to the upper stories, and in every room the visitor saw bewildering displays of furnishings, paintings, carvings, statuary, hangings and decorations, while a beautiful triple terrace garden composed the roof. Cost of the building was $80,000.

AN INTERESTING GROUP.—Those who were in attendance at the World's Fair will not fail to recognize the four views grouped above, elsewhere in this series fully described. At the top on the left is the Scandinavian restaurant, and next to it is the west side plaza showing one of the stairways leading to a station of the Intra-Mural Railway. Below, on the left, is a picture of the Japanese Hooden on Wooded Island, and to the right is the sham battle-ship Illinois, with the prow of Captain Anderson's Viking ship in view.

PLAZA IN FRONT OF MANUFACTURES BUILDING.—The view presented in the photograph comprehends a large section on the north side of the Grand Basin in front of Manufactures Hall. The Peristyle and its flanking colonnades are prominent features, emphasizing the colossal Statue of the Republic that rises in picturesque grandeur out of the east end of the Basin. The building seen on the left, next to the rostral column, is Music Hall, while to the extreme right of the colonnade is a corresponding structure known as the Casino. A great part of the section shown in the photograph was destroyed by fire on the night of January 8, 1894.

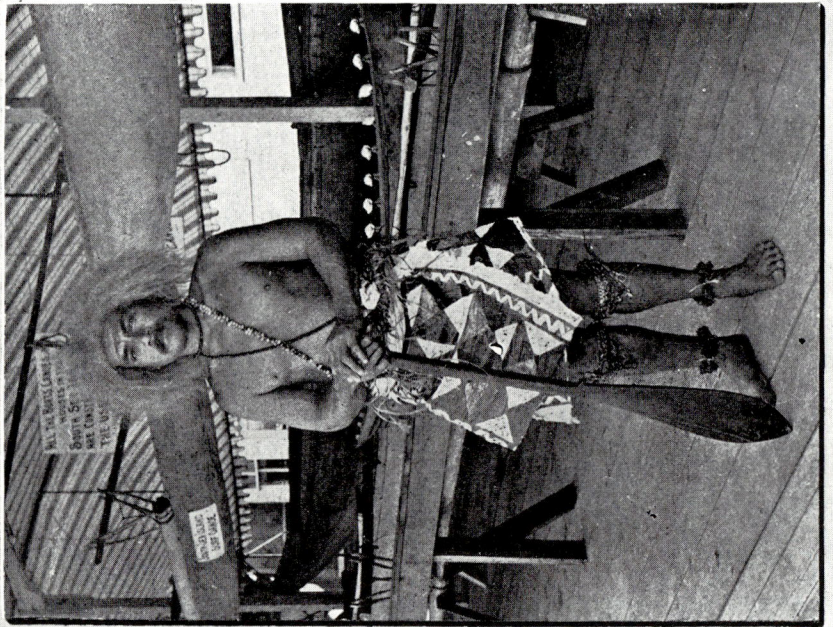
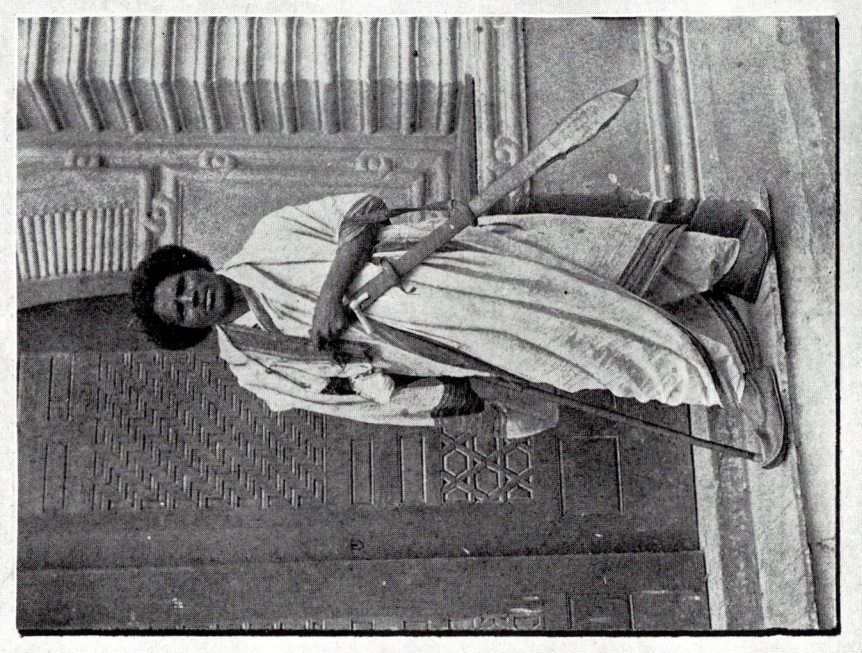

A FEW CHARACTERS IN THE MIDWAY.—The types shown in the photographs on this page represent, respectively, two Dahomey cannibals; a Samoan from Lupolo Island, dressed in a skirt of cocoanut fibre, and holding a canoe paddle in his hand; an Algerian miller, in the act of grinding rice between the two circular stones before him, and a Nubian warrior with a machete swung on his arm—about as dangerous a weapon as a garden hoe and not nearly so graceful.

THE GUATEMALA BUILDING.—Directly northeast of Brazil's Building, and nearby, was the more subdued and heavier appearing Spanish-like structure erected by the Government of Guatemala. In shape it was square, the four sides measuring 111 feet in length each. In the centre was a court 33 x 33, with a gallery extending around the interior in the form of a circular colonnade, affecting a style for centuries common in Palos. The four corners of the building were surmounted by handsomely decorated domes, rising to a height of 65 feet, and there was a roof terrace providing a splendid view of the grounds. A garden surrounded the building, planted with bananas, palms, coffee and other tropical growths. The building cost $40,000.

THE GERMAN GOVERNMENT BUILDING.—This towered and pinnacled structure was located on the lake front, near Spain's Building, and had a length of 150 feet with a depth of 175 feet. It presented a pleasing combination of styles, rather fancifully and mediævally diversified with turrets, balconies, bay-windows, and a tower reaching to the height of 150 feet. The main entrance simulated a chapel, over which was painted an ancient verse apotheosizing the Fatherland. The top portion of the tower was a belfry, in which three cast-steel bells were hung, weighing respectively 40, 60 and 80 hundredweight. The roof was covered with glazed tile of German importation, and the walls were of solid masonry, giving to the building an imposing and substantial appearance. Cost, $250,000.

A QUARTETTE OF PICTURESQUE BUILDINGS.—The views herewith have been particularly described in previous parts of "Magic City." The pictures show respectively the main, or central, entrance to California's State building; the west section of the Grand Basin; the towered and crenelated front of the Irish village; and the wall enclosing the German village and castle. Though on a small scale, the details are well brought out in these photographs, and the scope is satisfactory.

A GROUP OF STATE BUILDINGS.—The view herewith presents a section of the north part of the grounds, wherein we have glimpses of some of the State buildings there located. On the left, in the foreground, is the pillared porch of Nebraska's Building, while beyond are those of North Dakota and Kansas, the latter being one of very great attractiveness.

THE NORTH PROMENADE.—The above photograph pictures a beautiful promenade in the northeastern part of the Fair grounds, more charming because the large trees that stood in this portion of Jackson Park were preserved, while in many other sections they were removed. The location is easy to fix by those who visited the Exposition, as the Woman's Building is conspicuous on the left hand of the picture, while the Ferris Wheel in the distance shows that the view is looking directly west.

THE FISHERS CAUGHT.—In the Spanish section, West Court, of the Art Building was the realistic plaster photographed herewith, the work of A. Garcia y Marinas, a distinguished sculptor of Segovia. The subject is a horrible one, representing as it does a fisher boy and child in the dreadful grip of an octopus, that frightful monster with sinewy tentacles, gripping suckers, and hellish beak, which Victor Hugo has so fearfully described in his "Toilers of the Sea."

MIDWINTER FAIR ON DEDICATION DAY.—Dedication of the grounds took place on New Year's Day, but the official opening did not occur until January 27, upon which occasion the ceremonies were very impressive, and the attendance nearly 40,000 persons. The photograph herewith shows the appearance of the grounds at high noon on the day of dedication. On the left is the German Restaurant, and beyond is Administration Building and music pavilion. On the right, across the plaza, is the Allegoric Fountain, and in the background Agricultural and Horticultural Building. The day was a beautiful one, the crowds enthusiastic, and every augury seemed favorable to a very successful exposition, a prospect which flattered, but which was not, to every one's great regret, fully realized in point of attendance, but was exceeded in the completeness and diversity of the displays.

DEDICATION DAY AT THE MIDWINTER FAIR.—The scene pictured above represents the appearance of the plaza in front of Manufactures and Liberal Arts Building at noon of January 1, 1894, the day upon which the buildings were dedicated. In less than six months from the time that Hon. M. H. de Young, California's Commissioner to the World's Fair, conceived the idea of a Midwinter Exposition at San Francisco, Golden Gate Park, one of the beauty spots of the Far West, was covered with magnificent buildings, and the Fair was inaugurated, complete and under promising auspices. The attendance on this first day was 17,000, which was large considering the season, the times, and its opening almost upon the heels of the departing Chicago Fair. It was a stupendous undertaking, a happy enterprise, and in the highest degree creditable to the managers and to California.

OPENING-DAY CEREMONIES AT THE MIDWINTER FAIR.—The twenty-seventh day of January will henceforth be as famous in San Francisco's history as May 1 will ever continue to be in the history of Chicago. The photograph above represents Director-General M. H. de Young while in the act of addressing the people at the opening-day exercises of the Midwinter Fair. The attendance on that day was nearly 40,000 persons, a number large enough to indicate the great interest taken in the Fair by citizens of the State. The ceremonies were not so elaborate as those of a similar celebration at Chicago, but the enthusiasm was no less, and expectation was strengthened by the event to the point of great prediction as to the success of the enterprise.

THE ADMINISTRATION BUILDING.—California's Midwinter Fair occupied nearly 200 acres, and included seventy structures, of which number there were five main exposition buildings, and sixty-five subsidiary or auxiliary buildings. The general arrangement was around a Court of Honor, with the Administration Building occupying the centre. It was designed by Mr. A. Page Brown, and represents a combination of India and Siamese architecture—a style excessively florid, and to Americans curiously ornate. Exteriorly it was a central square surmounted with a dome, and four pavilions at the angles, each of which was crowned with a pineapple dome, beautifully colored. The richly ornate and decorated central dome was 50 feet in diameter and 125 feet in height, handsomely frescoed with allegoric paintings on the interior, and covered with incandescent lamps, by which it was gorgeously illuminated at night. In front was a superb fountain, elsewhere described.

MANUFACTURES AND LIBERAL ARTS BUILDING.—In architectural treatment Manufactures Building at the Midwinter Fair was much more graceful and ornate than its mammoth prototype at Chicago. It is doubtful if, in this utilitarian age, any other structure ever equaled it in gracefulness of proportion and beauty of detail. It was designed by Mr. A. Page Brown, of San Francisco, and was, of course, the largest structure on the grounds, its dimensions being 462 x 237 feet, about two and one-half acres. A feature of the building, after the plan of Manufactures Hall at Chicago, was a gallery thirty-five feet wide, which extended around the interior, upon which exhibits were made, and above this was a third floor, under the dome, from which steps led up to a roof garden, where a large display was made of palms, shrubbery and flowering plants. On the four corners of the building were roof balconies, richly adorned with specimens of Pacific Coast flora.

AGRICULTURAL BUILDING, MIDWINTER FAIR.—Agriculture and horticulture were assigned to a grand building giving glorious recognition to these twin industries, upon which the prosperity of our nation most largely depends. This really magnificent structure was designed by Mr. Samuel Newsom, who employed the old mission style of architecture with the most charming effects. The extreme length of the building was 266 feet 6 inches, and its greatest width 190 feet—a mammoth structure indeed. The centre rose in a colossal glass dome, crowned with a second dome, to a height of 90 feet, and the diameter was 100 feet. The main entrance was through three gracefully arched ways flanked by low towers, to the rears and flanks of which were two domes, that were specially picturesque features of the exterior view.

MECHANIC ARTS BUILDING AND ALLEGORIC FOUNTAIN.—The Hall of Mechanic Arts, or Machinery Building, was located opposite the Administration Building, between which was a delightful plaza with a superb centrepiece called the Allegoric Fountain. Machinery Hall was designed by Mr. Edward R. Swain, who likewise adopted the Oriental style to conform to the architecture of other main structures within the grounds. In size it was 324 x 160 feet, was covered by a terraced roof, and strangely decorated with slender prayer towers, while on the apex of the low central tower was the crescent of Islamism. The entrance was through a lofty arch, flanked by brilliantly colored kiosks, which produced a very pleasant impression upon visitors.

The Allegoric Fountain was a feature as prominent at the Midwinter Fair as the Statue of the Republic was at the Columbian Exposition. It was a rough pyramid of cement fifty feet high, surrounded at the base and covered with figures allegoric of California productions and industries. It had a double basin, the outer one of which was seventy-five feet in diameter and the inner one fifty feet.

FINE ARTS BUILDING, MIDWINTER FAIR.—The gem of Midwinter Fair structures was that herewith photographed—a splendid imitation of the best architecture of Egypt in the days of the Pharaohs. It was designed by Mr. C. C. McDougal, who, before commencing the plans, made an exhaustive study of the ruins of palaces at Philæ, Karnak, Luxor and history-preserved Memphis, and then embodied their most striking features in the building which is here shown. In size it was 120 x 60, with an extreme height, in the pyramidal dome, of 40 feet. Though constructed of perishable material, in appearance it was as solid as its ancient prototypes, and so handsome, as well as curious, it is a matter of very great regret that it will not endure as a permanent memorial of California's Great Exposition.

A CORNER OF THE FINE ARTS BUILDING.—The photograph herewith presents some of the details of the Fine Arts Building at the Midwinter Fair, showing its decorations of lotus columns, winged heads, repetition of sacred symbols on the cornices, representations of Osiris and hawk-headed Ra, images of priests, asps of royalty, solidity of appearance, absence of arches, and other characteristics of an Egyptian structure imitative of a Memphian palace. As such, it did not fail to command the studied attention of visitors.

ALAMEDA COUNTY BUILDING.—The enterprise of Californians was illustrated in many features of the Midwinter Fair. They entered heartily into the ambition to make their exposition not merely a success as a local affair, but to make it worthy to be called a national enterprise, reflecting credit upon all America. A splendid contribution to this end was the building herewith shown, erected by the people of Alameda County in which to make a display of their fields and workshops. The structure was of Spanish Renaissance style, 75 by 60 feet, and 40 feet high, with a balustraded roof promenade. Over the arched entrance rose a square open tower, covered with tile, and at the corners were pretty oriental spires, while other features aided to give to the building a very handsome appearance.

NORTHERN AND CENTRAL CALIFORNIA BUILDING.—A very handsome and spacious structure was that erected through contributions made by people living in Central and Northern California, in which to make special displays of the products of these sections. There was no pretence of architectural embellishment in the building, yet its appearance was pleasing, and its adaptation to the purpose intended was perfect. The structure was 70 x 50 feet, one story, and had for its chief features a long, pillared porch, and an arched glass roof which flooded the interior with light. The gabled front was two stories, so as to provide rooms for visitors and the officers having the displays in charge.

The thirty-four sketch photographs presented in the above group charmingly illustrate what was perhaps the most interesting feature of the Midwinter Fair. Californians are justly proud of the history of their State, because she has attained her greatness through difficulties which could only be mastered by the brave and adventurous pioneers who wrested the territory from Mexico and constructed a commonwealth, grand, great, powerful as she is. They love to think of the transition days of '49 and '50, when Yuba Dam was merging into San Francisco; when Mexican fandangoes were giving place to the American shin-dig; when poverty was changing her pesetas for gold dollars, and things generally were open wide. These hey-day scenes it was desirable to re-enact at the Fair, and the photographs above represent how completely this ambition was realized. There is shanty and shack, log-cabin saloon, dance house, stage coach, view of mountain scenery, place where gold was found by Marshall, miner's home in the deep forest, toll road, and a corps of female dancers that were dear to the miner's heart, because there was such a severe scarcity of skirts in the early days.

DISPLAY IN SANTA CLARA COUNTY'S BUILDING.—Santa Clara County is probably the richest district in California, famous alike for its wheat, wines and orchards. Our photograph represents the interior of Santa Clara County's Building at the Midwinter Fair, with its splendid exhibits of wines, olive oil and preserved fruits. In the centre is an heroic figure of an armored knight mounted upon a spirited steed panoplied for battle. This effigy is made entirely of prunes grown in Santa Clara County, these fruits being used not only in forming the horse and rider, but they likewise compose the shield, helmet, plume, sword and bridle, a work of great ingenuity.

THE WALNUT ELEPHANT FROM LOS ANGELES COUNTY.—Many of the counties of California were represented at the Midwinter Fair by special buildings in which displays of their respective products were made. The photograph above exhibits in curious design one of the industries of Los Angeles County, where the raising of walnuts, grapes, oranges, almonds and olives has become, in the last few years, more extensive than in any other part of the world. The Walnut Elephant proved to be a very attractive feature of the Fair, and was an effective advertisement for the county that produced it.

TOLL HOUSE IN THE '49 MINING CAMP.—"The days of old, the days of gold," were illustrated by a mining camp located under a panoramic view of Mount Shasta within the Fair grounds. On one side of the street was a tavern, blacksmith shop, dance house and miners' cabins; the other side was lined up with a big gambling house, store and saloons. A little way up the street was a stream of water, where sluicing and panning was done, illustrating the art of gathering gold. A stage-coach traversed the street, and pistols were not conspicuous by their absence. The entrance to this strange exposition of early times in California was through the toll house pictured above.

SANTA BARBARA'S BUILDING AND THE FIRTH WHEEL.—Santa Barbara County erected a building imitative of an Egyptian pyramid, while Santa Barbara City people were specially represented by the structure above photographed. It was called "The Amphibion," because it contained large tanks in which sea lions and sea tigers were exhibited for a small admission price. A popular feature near the Amphibion was the Firth Wheel shown in the photograph. It was built after the structural plan of the Ferris Wheel, but was 100 feet less in diameter. But carrying people to a height of 150 feet, and equipped with sixteen cars, the wheel was a great wonder, and received liberal patronage.

A PRAIRIE SCHOONER OF 1850.—The old wagon here photographed is a relic and realistic reminder of early days in California, in which goods of many kinds were hauled overland by means of ox-teams from Leavenworth to Yuba Dam, the name by which the city of San Francisco was first known. This old wagon, if it could but use its tongue to speak, might tell many a tale of adventure with Indians on the plains, and hardships in the mountains over which it was slowly drawn by famishing oxen, driven by desperate men. Wagons of this kind were built for the hardest service and to carry a load of 6000 pounds. Along the way were relays of cattle, and at the heavy grades as many as ten yokes of oxen were required, so that overland freighting was a business in which a great deal of capital was employed, yet the rates were so enormous that the business yielded immense profit.

CYCLORAMA OF HAWAII'S VOLCANO OF KILAUEA.—A very popular attraction at the Midwinter Fair was a cyclorama 200 feet in diameter realistically representing the great burning volcano of Kilauea. This is one of the largest volcanoes of the world, the crater of which is eight miles in circumference and from 800 to 1500 feet deep. It is on the island of Hawaii, and is constantly active, though not in violent eruption since 1840. The cyclorama was located within the space allotted to Hawaii, and proved to be an attraction of great popularity, not alone because of its fiery magnificence, the marvel of its realism, but also because of the political prominence which Hawaii has recently gained. Within the enclosure was also a Sandwich Island theatre, where the Huluhula dance, first described by Capt. Cook, was performed by native girls. There were also huts of cocoanut palm, Hawaiian displays, and a company of natives, in the village, a photograph of which is presented above.

SCENE IN THE JAPANESE VILLAGE.—The Japanese buildings in the section of Oriental Concessions at the Midwinter Fair were different in many respects from those constructed by these people at Chicago, being lighter, and exhibiting a somewhat different order of architecture, as is seen by the above photograph. The situation of the buildings at the San Francisco Fair was also more picturesque, the climate and native vegetation permitting of charming decoration and delightful surroundings. The thatched bamboo building in the foreground was a tea house, and the larger one in the background represented a temple, in which, however, some of the Japanese made their temporary quarters.

CHILCAT INDIANS.—A company of twenty Chilcat Indians, composed of men, women and children, direct from the Chilcat country of Alaska, were an interesting feature of the Midwinter Fair. They occupied a temporary village enclosed by a woven grass fence, and their habitations were likewise made of grass, thatched sufficiently to protect the occupants from rain. These people have undergone a great change in their manner of living during the past thirty years, or since Alaska became a possession of the United States. Their principal occupation is salmon-fishing, selling their catches to canneries established by whites in their country. Being thus brought into contact with British and Americans, they show the result of new environments by adopting the clothes of civilization, though their religious superstitions remain practically as before.

THE INDIAN VILLAGE.—The fragmentary tribes of Indians who live in California, Arizona and Nevada were represented at the Midwinter Fair, and were on exhibition to visitors within a high board enclosure. None of the blanket Indians were brought to San Francisco, because they belong to the central region, east of the Rocky Mountains. Those in the village photographed are so far civilized that they have adopted the clothes of white people, and are engaged as farmers, miners and fruit raisers, thus demonstrating that at least some Indians are amenable to law, and under proper conditions may adopt civilized ways. Their summer huts are shown on the right, comfortable enough in warm weather; but these Indians are industrious enough to build log cabins when they find employment or place suitable for permanent residence.

CACTUS PLANTS IN THE MOQUI INDIAN VILLAGE.—There are nowhere else in the world greater vegetable curiosities than grow in the arid regions of Arizona and Southern California. Examples of the colossal cacti that were transplanted from the great southwest desert to the Midwinter Fair are shown in the photograph. The tallest specimen thus shown is thirty-five feet, and three feet in diameter, a vegetable giant armed with spines dangerous to touch. Other smaller varieties are also shown, and it will be noticed that a paling fence is imitated by the use of cucumber cacti plants. This remarkable exhibition is in the Moqui Indian village of the Fair, and is worth many miles of travel to see, as every variety native to this country is to be found in the collection. In the foreground of the picture are three Moqui Indians and an Indian child. They very greatly resemble Mexican peons.

AN ESQUIMAUX WOMAN AND BABE.—The photograph herewith is of an Esquimaux woman and her four-day-old infant, born in the village of her people at the Midwinter Fair. A peculiarity among uncivilized people is the fact that maternity is accompanied by neither pain nor weakness, hence it is no matter of surprise that this woman was able to receive visitors and show her wee babe in swaddling clothes, appreciative as she was of the acute desire upon the part of white people to see infants of uncivilized mothers, and their willingness to pay well for the privilege. This desire she turned to good profit, by holding a levee for curious visitors through all hours of the day. The skirt and dress hanging on the inner walls of the cabin were gifts to the woman, who retains them as hut decorations, rather than subject them to the uses of wear.

ENTRANCE TO THE ESQUIMAUX VILLAGE.—The photograph above admirably shows a portion of the front of the Esquimaux village at the Midwinter Fair. The principal objects of interest in the picture are, of course, the two little, chubby, Esquimaux children perched on the shelf of the ticket office. It is proper to state that one of these is a boy and the other a girl, but the distinction of sex is not plain to visitors, hence the children are a source of much guessing. Esquimaux clothe all their children in like garments of bear and seal skin, as they are seen in the photograph, nor is there any distinction in the dress of men and women during the winter season in the extreme northern latitude of their ice dwellings.

POPULAR CULTURE IN AMERICA

1800-1925

An Arno Press Collection

Alger, Jr., Horatio. **Making His Way; Or Frank Courtney's Struggle Upward.** n. d.

Bellew, Frank. **The Art of Amusing:** Being a Collection of Graceful Arts, Merry Games, Odd Tricks, Curious Puzzles, and New Charades. 1866

Browne, W[illiam] Hardcastle. **Witty Sayings By Witty People.** 1878

Buel, J[ames] W[illiam]. **The Magic City:** A Massive Portfolio of Original Photographic Views of the Great World's Fair and Its Treasures of Art . . . 1894

Buntline, Ned [E. Z. C. Judson]. **Buffalo Bill; And His Adventures in the West.** 1886

Camp, Walter. **American Football.** 1891

Captivity Tales. 1974

Carter, Nicholas [John R. Coryell]. **The Stolen Pay Train.** n. d.

Cheever, George B. **The American Common-Place Book of Poetry,** With Occasional Notes. 1831

Sketches and Eccentricities of Colonel David Crockett, of West Tennessee. 1833

Evans, [Wilson], Augusta J[ane]. **St. Elmo: A Novel.** 1867

Finley, Martha. **Elsie Dinsmore.** 1896

Fitzhugh, Percy Keese. **Roy Blakeley On the Mohawk Trail.** 1925

Forester, Frank [Henry William Herbert]. **The Complete Manual For Young Sportsmen.** 1866

Frost, John. **The American Speaker:** Containing Numerous Rules, Observations, and Exercises, on Pronunciation, Pauses, Inflections, Accent and Emphasis . . . 1845

Gauvreau, Emile. **My Last Million Readers.** 1941

Haldeman-Julius, E[manuel]. **The First Hundred Million.** 1928

Johnson, Helen Kendrick. **Our Familiar Songs and Those Who Made Them.** 1909

Little Blue Books. 1974

McAlpine, Frank. **Popular Poetic Pearls,** and Biographies of Poets. 1885

McGraw, John J. **My Thirty Years in Baseball.** 1923

Old Sleuth [Harlan Halsey]. **Flyaway Ned; Or, The Old Detective's Pupil. A Narrative of Singular Detective Adventures.** 1895

Pinkerton, William A[llan]. **Train Robberies, Train Robbers, and the "Holdup" Men.** 1907

Ridpath, John Clark. **History of the United States,** Prepared Especially for Schools. Grammar School Edition, 1876

The Tribune Almanac and Political Register for 1876. 1876

Webster, Noah. **An American Selection of Lessons in Reading and Speaking.** Fifth Edition, 1789

Whiteman, Paul and Mary Margaret McBride. **Jazz.** 1926

5772 7034 14 MAB
04/07/05

save
cover